"The Soul
of
Belly Dance"
'Culture and History'

Edited by Mezdulene Bliss

For information or special orders please contact:
mezdulene@mezdulene.com
Or write:
Mezdulene
P.O. Box 680
Sutherlin, Oregon 97479

ISBN-13:978-1500160890

ISBN-10:150016089X

Dedicated to Halima
Thank you for your enduring friendship, and for sharing the dance with me, the movements, the history and the joy.

CONTENTS

PREFACE:

I wanted to share with you how this wonderful book came about.

Jareeda was a magazine for over thirty years. Yes! It was the longest running belly dance periodical in the world and was subscribed to by dancers all over the planet.

I was the editor for almost twenty years and over that time met so many amazing dancers. Some of them have become friends over the years. I loved going to events and meeting people in person whom I had met through Jareeda by letters and then by emails.

In 2012, I was at a large event and spoke with two amazing dancers about the future of Jareeda. One of them suggested turning Jareeda into a book. She said, "As soon as the magazine is printed it's out of date, but a book will live on forever." I loved her idea, but I wasn't sure how to accomplish it.

Less than three months later, I was struck down by an illness that lasted over five months. I was unable to work and had a whole lot of time to just think. Of course I worried and worried about the magazine getting more and more behind, and then one day, I woke up with an inspirational type vision where I knew the answer.

"The Soul of Belly Dance" is Jareeda's very first book! I was so nervous about telling subscribers about the change, but when I did, I received nothing but support. With all the notes I received, only one said they would miss the magazine even though they were looking forward to the book. Everyone was encouraging and enthusiastic, so I know I made the right decision.

And, when I asked for contributors, again I received so much support! What a wonderful experience this has been.

Thanks to Kickstarter.com, I was able to raise the funds for this new beginning and you will see in the back of the book a list of those supporters.

There is no limit to my gratitude for everyone who has helped make this possible. It's truly a dream come true.

May each of you who reads this book be inspired to live your own dance dreams.

FORWARD:

We've all been drawn to belly dancing by something. Maybe it was for exercise, an attraction to the costumes, the desire to perform. Maybe it was just your friend inviting you to attend a class with her. For whatever reason you started dancing, there is something deeper that kept you dancing.

I call this, the soul of belly dance. It's this deeper aspect of the dance, the history, the culture the feeling inside of us, that seems to get into our blood like a sacred calling that we've answered and continue to honor. It's an unseen force of women dancing throughout the ages and throughout the world, the knowing that we are connected in a time and space continuum to our sister dancers. It's about an art form that has traveled through time from the ancient to the present changing and morphing, never limited or bound by societal constraints.

Wherever I travel, I know that if I contact dancers in the area I'm visiting, they'll be happy to meet me, invite me to teach, to dance or just to go to lunch. The dance connects us on an almost subconscious level, in a meaningful way that is hard to describe yet easy to experience.

It is my belief, born from feeling not actual knowledge, that our dance pre-dates written history. We all know that ancient cultures worshipped the divine feminine. It was the woman who created life, who grew a new human being inside of her and then after giving birth nourishing the baby with the food her body provided. The lineage of a person was traced through the mother's side of the family. After all, everyone knew who gave birth to them.

As a child I gained a sense of an ancient culture being brought into modern times. I was raised on the San Carlos Apache Reservation in Arizona. The Apaches are still a matriarchal society, and they dance to nothing more than drumming and chanting. When a girl comes of age, they have a week-long celebration. Their dances and chants have been passed down through time from the ancient to the present. In fact, the chants are so ancient that they no longer understand the words because their language has changed over what is probably thousands of years. They do know the essence of each chant, and that each one celebrates a different aspect of life, birth, death, marriage, healing, coming out, hunting success and so forth.

The Apaches have never had a written language, so everything is verbally passed to the next generation.

Because I had this experience, it only makes sense to me that the same thing happened all over the world. Beliefs, stories, songs, music and dance were passed from generation to generation long before the written word was developed.

So, it's no stretch of the imagination that women have danced since ancient times. To this day in the Middle East many women still dance to clapping, drumming and chanting. There is no need for fancy musical equipment, just the supportive gathering of people making music through hands and voices.

To me, our dance is a celebration of the divine feminine. I used to hate the term 'belly dance' until I got in touch with myself as a woman through the art of belly dance. It is a woman's dance, and as a woman, we have the ability to grow life inside of our belly, to cradle this new life in our pelvis between our hips and to nourish this life with our breasts. As I dance with my hips and rib cage, undulate my belly and torso, I feel my power as a woman and when I perform I feel a loving feminine essence flowing through me and out into the audience.

After dancing for ten years, I gave birth to my son. When he went into distress, I pushed him out in three pushes. Three pushes! I have never felt more powerful as a woman!

This is my experience. The dance has empowered me, has helped me get in touch with the strength of my femininity, has touched me to my core. In essence, it has changed my life and has been the source of a depth of healing beyond imagination.

This book is a celebration of the soul of the dance, that deep and enduring, meaningful aspect of our beautiful art form. I hope that you enjoy reading it and that you are educated and inspired, that it gives you pause for thought and helps you connect even more deeply to your beautiful and divine self.

Whirling –

from the dervishes of Turkey to the Tanoura dancers in Egypt
By Nicole McLaren

A dance could not be any more contradictory. The Whirling Dance lingers between spectacular show and meditation in motion; it combines trance and technique. A surprising paradox, unified like lovers within the dance. This one-of-a-kind fusion is the reason why, as a performing art, the stage variation of the old Turkish whirling rite inherits a special place within the Oriental Dance styles.

In general, turns bear something very original, something genuine; something very archaic. Kids spin playfully around their axis until they fall to the floor, giggling. They enjoy the sensual experience of a temporary loss of orientation. In physics, mathematics, literature or philosophy turns, circular concepts, wheels and cycles are omnipresent in many sciences and art forms. Especially in dance, first and foremost in Ballet or Ice skating, repetitive turns belong to the fundamental movement repertoire. Yet, dance of all sorts celebrate the great aesthetics of the turn in all its grandeur. Is there a dance style at all which knows no turns?

A dervish whirls for hours
The spinning of the whirling dervishes of Konya in Turkey, rose to worldwide popularity. It is an integral part of their religious ceremony "Sema," which means "listening," or "listening within." During this rite they turn, *sometimes for hours*, around their own axis. While the dervishes whirl, their awareness focuses inward. The trancelike effect, which constant whirling may cause, brings the dervishes (or Sufis, according to Sufism, the mystical movement within Islam) in religious ecstasy closer to Allah.

Sufis strive for a mystical experience of the divine: the Unio Mystica, a union with the divine, a state of oneness with God. It illustrates one of the key concepts of Sufism which according to the Sufistic doctrine everything is; we all are part of the great whole. The dervishes of Konya experience this belief within the whirling rite.

"Come whoever you are"
Also in the case of an audience present, for the Sufis, the whirling is less an outer performance than the sharing of a mutual experience. They consider the audience as true participators of the ceremony. Therefore, the spectators should not clap at the end of the rite. Hereby they would state that they do not belong to the ceremony, but are mere outsiders watching the whirlers "perform." Consequently, this would represent a dualistic vantage which goes against the Sufistic credo of everything being part of a greater whole.

Throughout the centuries, Sufis sometimes faced repression because of their beliefs. Some considered their way of life and religious approaches as inadequate; for example, music being played during religious ceremonies was considered a worldly approach. The great Persian Sufi poet Rumi, whom the order of the Whirling dervishes traces back to, sparked additional resentment by his famous quote, "Come, come, whoever you are." Opponents considered these words as heretic, because they could be interpreted as showing a tolerance to other religions.

In 1925, Mustafa Kemal Atatürk, the first President of Turkey, wanted to modernize his country and model it into a more western-orientated state. Consequently, he made all Islamic brotherhoods illegal, including the Mevlevi order (the Whirling dervishes). Basically, this order is still illegal, even though in 1954 the practice was partially allowed again; the whirling ceremony turned out to be very lucrative, as it allured innumerable tourists.

Rumi inspired Goethe and Madonna
Rumi, who lived in Turkey from 1207 to 1273 A.D., initiated the whirling rite, which the Sufis of the Mevlevi order still practice.

It is said that Rumi once wandered through a market in Konya, and heard the beating of a hammer smith. Within the beats, he thought he heard the words "La ilaha illa-llah," one of the most important of suwar(verses) in the Quran. Deeply moved he spread out his arms and started whirling. **Editor's Note: "La Ilaha illa-llah" can be translated into English as meaning, "There is no god, but God/Allah."**

Rumi left behind a huge heritage also affecting other fields: As a poet he created a great lyrical opus in his Persian mother tongue, beyond "The Great Divan." His poetry affected people worldwide, and throughout the centuries. Rumi inspired the great German writer Goethe, who wrote, "West-Eastern Diwan." The UNESCO honoured Rumi in 2007 because of his 800th birthday, and pop singer Madonna used Rumi's lyrics in her song, "Bittersweet" in 1998. The Turkish musician Mercan Dede named his first album "Sufi Dreams," and in 2007 released the album, "800," he called it his birthday cake for Rumi.

The Dance with the Tanoura
Whirling Dance for the stage is not to be mixed up with the religious Whirling rite of the dervishes. Some Sufis feel offended if they are called "dancers." For them, Whirling is religious meditation. On the contrary, a dancer on stage performs in order to please an audience. Therefore, one may avoid the term "dervish dancer" when referencing the stylized stage variation.

The Egyptians adapted the whirling technique of the Dervishes in Turkey and it grew into a one-of-a-kind stage art form. The extremely popular dance with the tanoura, the Arabian term for "skirt," is a performance for an audience; the Whirlers usually don't belong to a Sufi order. Also, the tanoura underlines the show aspect: a full-circle skirt often made of a very colorful fabric. Sewn into the rim is a hemp rope, rubber or a chain, so the skirt will unfold with whirling, thanks to the centrifugal force, and will hover like a plate. Often, the tanoura is multilayered, and sometimes the dancers wear multiple colorful tanouras simultaneously. Highly skilled and popular tanoura artists of today, include names like Ziya Azazi from Turkey/Austria or Bondok from Egypt/Germany.

Embrace dizzyness, release control
The music for the Whirling dance on stage is sometimes inspired by the Sufi music, and creates a mesmerizing atmosphere. The rhythm which is often used is the 2/4 Rhythm Ayub or Zaar rhythm (Dum – Tak Dum Tak). Often a ney, a reed flute and one of the central instruments in Sufi music, is used. They say that its soulful and melancholic tone portrays the flute's great sorrow of having been cut out of the reed it came from, and its deep longing of being unified again with its origin. This metaphor of striving for a reconnection beautifully expresses the Sufistic idea of everything being part of a greater whole.

For the Whirling Dance, paradoxically, it is extremely important to consciously release control. The dancer strives for a dedication to the whirling experience, and the sensual effect coming along with it; a temporary disorientation, a sensation of letting go, of letting loose. This is a challenge, physically, as well as mentally. On the one hand, because dancers, in particular, try to achieve the greatest body control possible. On the other hand, the constant and repetitive whirling move is new to them and might somehow feel odd for the body. Consequently, some dancers might get dizzy in the beginning – while others won't feel anything at all. If someone experiences dizziness and embraces it, rather than fighting it, it helps to overcome it. Ultimately, once the feeling of a possible initial discomfort is left behind, the Whirling experience may bless the dancer with an overwhelmingly intense awareness of the moment – a simultaneous sensation of great calm and euphoric joy.

Whirling with a burning tanoura
Initially one might think a whirling choreography for the stage wouldn't be complex, but rather, plain and simple. A differentiated view unfolds a great variety of possibilities, though. The dancer can combine calm and meditative elements with spectacular show moves with the tanoura. Besides using torso and hips, smooth and fluent arm moves, and wild head turns, there are different whirling techniques; jumping, skipping, hopping on one leg. They may skillfully integrate the whole space of the stage, whirling fast and slow, dynamically and steadily. Additionally, if she uses black light or LED lights sewn directly into the tanoura. And, of course, nearly endless possibilities of props, which can be combined creatively with the tanoura: drums, veils, zills, swords, Isis wings, Tibetan sleeves or Chinese ribbons.

Furthermore, the tanoura presents a wide array of possibilities: The so-called wheel, either at hip, shoulder or over-head height, evokes wowing effects. In order to create it, the dancer holds the tanoura in a certain way so the skirt will hover diagonally around her. Moreover, the dancer can take off the tanoura, fold it to the popular "baby," use it as a cape, whirl it around single handedly, throw it high into the air, and let it waver down unto her. Or she lights the rim of a special pyro tanoura and spectacularly whirls in a ring of fire. Using all these possibilities – and with a playful "jester's licence" state of mind, so many more are yet to be explored – a dedicated dancer can choreograph outstandingly creative performances. The stage is beckoning!

Whirling within a dance routine

Within the Oriental Dance scene, Whirling Dance has not yet become a mass phenomenon, although the ability of spinning around their own axis vastly enhances the skills of an oriental dancer and ameliorates their repertoire. A dancer who masters constant whirling, will seamlessly, and seemingly effortlessly, cope with a lot of fast, consecutive spins, which are very popular in the great finale of a classical dance routine. The deep aesthetics of the whirling movement only unfolds its full beauty, if the dancer is able to completely devote herself to these turns, staying grounded and centered, with a strong inner axis and an upright composure.

Besides the refinement of the dancing skills, Whirling Dance also broadens the spectrum of styles within a show, and enriches its diversity. On many big stages, the Whirling Dance is still rarely seen – hence, the effects of the danced turns unroll all the more.

A paradox, unified within the dance

Within the oriental dance styles, the Whirling dance is often accredited to having a certain, exceptional position. Although the stage variation went a long way from its ceremonial Sufi origins, whirling still blends performance and meditation, skills, and spirit. The dancer may find, seemingly contradictorily, great calmness within the movement.

Generally, the Whirling Dance combines an enthralling set of oppositions. It is a spectacular stage dance, but at the same time often focuses inward, striving for immersion; self-absorption. It creates a deep deliberation, while the body simultaneously is in full motion; it bears meditative calmness and rousing joy of life. Its ambiance harmoniously meanders and can be as playful and strong, or as sublime and solemn. It raises the awareness of the moment, while the whirler journeys to their very self.

For a dancer, whirling is an exceedingly sensual experience; intense, delightful, and even trancelike. For the audience though, the one-of-a-kind mystic atmosphere, the forceful energy, and at the same time, hypnotizing inwardness, mesmerizes the spectators. This unique art of dance lingers between control and letting go, between trance and technique. It seems to touch the invisible, a dance that has the power to enchant – like a secret of another world.

Nicole McLaren

Nicole McLaren is an international dance artist who performs worldwide: Egypt, America, Germany, Austria, France, Italy, the Netherlands, or South Africa. The Swiss dancer, intsructor and choreographer for Oriental Dance with special focus on Whirling dance (Tanoura) lives in Zurich (Switzerland) and Los Angeles (USA). She also performs to the live music of the Oriental Gypsy band Ssassa or to the one of her own band Harlekin. Besides dancing, she is a Karate Black Belt and has competed for years in European and World Championships, in which she won bronze and silver medals. Professionally, Nicole graduated from the University of Zurich with a double Master of Arts.

Nicole fell in love with one particular type of oriental dance style: Whirling. For her, this highly dynamic dance bears a unique, mesmerizing quality, paradoxically a great calmness while being in full motion. It simultaneously embraces a deep meditative tranquility and a vibrant joy of life. In her very own Whirling style, Nicole combines modern music and dance elements as well as props from different cultures with the original Turkish whirling technique. Additionally to the Egyptian Tanoura she uses Middle Eastern veils and Western wings, traditional Tibetan sleeves, or Chinese silk ribbons in her Whirling on stage. Consequently, the dance performance blends elements from various cultures and time periods and thus unifies past and present in order to create a new, contemporary stage form of the Whirling Dance.
www.nicolemclaren.com

The Origin of Belly Dancing?

By Shira

As students start to learn about *raqs* (the Arabic word for dancing), one of the most natural questions to ask is, "What are the origins of this dance?" The Internet is full of conflicting information on this subject, and it can be hard for newcomers to the dance to sort out fact from fantasy.

The true origins of this dance are lost in time. Anthropologists have never found an ancient diary stating, "Today I invented a new dance that uses hip drops, shimmies, and undulations. The reason I did it was ___," nor is it reasonable to expect that such a diary will ever be found. Many dancers in the U.S. today refer to the dance form as "the oldest dance," but there is no evidence that *raqs* technique is any older than any other type of human movement.

Origin theories often reveal more about the people who believe those theories than they do about the actual history of the dance. Below are some of the more widely-believed origin theories, with insight into where they came from.

Origin Theory #1: Seducing Men

The origin theory most common among the U.S. general public is that of women using *raqs* to compete for the attentions of the Sultan; or, more generally, the notion of a dance of seduction. This belief can be traced to the 19th and early 20th centuries, when the pop culture of the time was heavily influenced by the Orientalism of the era.

The Orientalist movement in art, which flourished in the 19th century, featured many images of nude women, often painted by artists who had never visited the Middle East. As noted by Linda Nochlin in her essay "The Imaginary Orient", "Like many other art works of its time, [Jean-Léon] Gérôme's Orientalist painting [*Slave Market*] managed to bring forth two ideological assumptions about power: one about men's power over women; the other about white men's superiority to, hence justifiable control over, inferior, darker races, precisely those who indulge in this sort of regrettably lascivious commerce." In other words, not only were such paintings the pornography of their day, but they also served as political propaganda to justify Europe's violent efforts to colonize North Africa. A number of images from this period depicted semi-nude women dancing for the male gaze, including Gérôme's 1863 *Dance of the Almeh*, Gérôme's 1873 *Almeh Performing the Sword Dance*, Gustav Moreau's 1875 *Salomé Dancing Before Herod*, and Moreau's 1876 *Apparition*.

Visual arts were not the only facet of European culture to use themes from the East to titillate the public's appetite for nudity.

[1] "The Imaginary Orient", an essay in *The Politics of Vision*. By Linda Nochlin. Page 45.

Oscar Wilde's play Salomé, which was published in the 1890's, drew inspiration from Moreau's paintings of a sensuous nude Salomé. Wilde took the idea a step further by introducing a "dance of the seven veils" into the story line. Richard Strauss turned Wilde's play into an opera which made its debut in 1905 in Dresden, Germany, and within 2 years had been performed in 50 other opera houses. The nudity of the dance scene outraged many wealthy theater patrons, but at the same time created a pop culture phenomenon known as "Salomania."

In the early 20th century, entertainers in North America were fascinated by the idea of the Turkish harem, filled with beauties to be enjoyed by one man alone. Songs, movies, and plays were written that drew on this theme. Often, these lyrics referenced the seductive dance being performed in the harem.

For example, Irving Berlin's 1913 song "In My Harem," contains lyrics saying, "And the dance they do will make you wish that you were in a harem." The 1931 song "Egyptian Ella" spoke of Ella, a dancer who was popular with the men, including lyrics such as, "So the Pash wrote her a royal note with his royal fist, it said because of the dance she does, she's on his royal waiting list."

The imagery of a sinuous dancer performing for a man's pleasure frequently appears in motion pictures and animated cartoons of the 20th century. Sometimes the man is watching openly, as in the Sultan in the Mighty Mouse cartoon *The Sultan's Birthday*. Other times, the man is a voyeur, such as Woody Woodpecker peering into a tent in the cartoon *Socko in Morocco*. More recently, such scenes have appeared in the movie *Charlie Wilson's War* and the "Homer's Night Out" episode of *The Simpsons*. The scenes occur so frequently in entertainment media that people don't think to question them.

The notion of beautiful women in the Turkish harem using dance to compete for the Sultan's attention may serve as an attractive sexual fantasy, but historical fact is much more mundane. In the Ottoman harems, the women had very little contact with the Sultan. Usually, his mother or his first wife chose whom to send to his bed, rather than the Sultan himself making the decision.

It was common for young girls entering the harem to be trained in music, dance, or other performing arts if they showed the aptitude. Although they would occasionally perform for the Sultan, more commonly they performed for the other women of the harem.

In her memoirs of what it was like to live in the Imperial Harem of Turkey, author Leyla (Saz) Hanimefendi wrote, "[raqs] is hardly favored in Turkey and certainly a dance in the Imperial Serail never takes a provocative, lascivious, or indecent form which the Westerners imagine it to have and which can be seen performed in their own countries by dancers more or less Oriental. The actual belly dance is really a dance of Arabic origin."

Men's magazines of the 1950's kept alive the stereotypes of *raqs* dancers. The May 1953 issue of *Foto-Rama* magazine featured a photograph on page 35 of Samia Gamal wearing a sweater, airbrushed to add prominent nipples. This was part of a 3-page layout titled "Samia Gamal: The Girl Who Shook the Pyramids." The November 18, 1953 issue of *People Today* magazine featured a 3-page photo layout of Nejla Ates wearing pasties instead of a costume bra. Other men's magazines featured sexy dancers as characters in spy thrillers and detective stories.

With centuries of entertainment media selling artwork, motion pictures, magazines, and television shows featuring *raqs* dancers doing sexy performances for the pleasure of men, it's no wonder that the general public in North America continues to cling to this origin theory.

[2] *The New Penguin Opera Guide.* By Amanda Holden.
[3] *The Imperial Harem of the Sultans: Daily Life at the Çiragan Palace During the 19th Century.* By Leyla (Saz) Hanimefendi. Page 50.

Origin Theory #2: "The Oldest Dance" as Birth Ritual

This theory asserts that raqs originated as an exercise to assist women in labor with the delivery of babies. It was originally proposed by the dancer Morocco in an article titled "Belly Dancing and Childbirth" which appeared in the April 1965 issue of *Sexology*. This article stated, "Oriental dancing, as the Arabs themselves call it, is one of the oldest forms of dance, originating with pre-Biblical religious rites worshiping motherhood and having as its practical side the preparation of females for the stresses of childbirth. Thus it is the oldest form of natural childbirth instruction."

Other writers later added their own interpretation to Morocco's theory, including Jamila Salimpour in her 1979 book *Belly Dance: The Birth Magic Ritual* and Daniela Gioseffi in her 1980 book *Earth Dancing, Mother Nature's Oldest Rite*. La Meri stated in her 1977 book *Total Education in Ethnic Dance*, "[Belly dance] is a relatively recent development, stemming from an ancient ritual performed only in the chamber of a woman in childbirth."

In her original 1965 article, Morocco identified three sources to support her theory: 1) an interview with a woman from Saudi Arabia who said that in the 1950's women in certain remote rural areas would gather around a woman in labor and ritualistically perform movements reminiscent of those done in Oriental dance; 2) A passage in *The Dancer of Shamahka* by Armen Ohanian in which she refers to *raqs* as "our poem of the mystery and pain of motherhood", and 3) the practices of a small sect of Allaoui Muslims which link Oriental dance movement to childbirth. Morocco's article presents no concrete evidence to justify a claim of "one of the oldest forms of dance" or "pre-Biblical religious rites worshiping motherhood."

The theory was very much an idea of its time. It provided a tool for responding to criticism from multiple sources, primarily from those who believed the dance's origin to lie in pleasing men. It dissociated the dance from the sexy image depicted in men's magazines of the 1950's and linked it to concepts that were much easier to defend to the prevailing cultural mentality, those of female empowerment and giving birth.

Some of the women involved in the feminist movement of the era rejected Oriental dance on the grounds that it pandered to traditional female roles of trying to please men. In her article "Feminism and Belly Dance," Andrea Deagon reported that, following a presentation she did on *raqs* in the early 1980's for her dormitory's arts series, an audience member said, "I consider myself a feminist, and I was offended by what you just did. I was surprised we'd even have something like this in our arts series."

Navigating between the wishful fantasies of men who enjoyed the "dance of seduction" origin story and the female-empowerment agenda of feminism, dancers found the balance they were seeking in the myth of *raqs* originating from birth ritual. This theory celebrated an activity that was uniquely feminine (giving birth) while dismissing as unimportant the desire of men to believe that anything a woman did was for the purpose of pleasing them.

[4] *Total Education in Ethnic Dance*. By Russell Meriwether Hughes. Page 67.
[5] "Feminism and Belly Dance." By Andrea Deagon. Published in *Habibi* Volume 17, Number 4 (Winter 1999).

The only problem: there was no proof.

It's impossible to discern which came first, *raqs* or some sort of dance that involved running and leaping, acrobatics, arm-waving, or other movement. Therefore, it's not reasonable to assert that *raqs* is "the oldest dance." Perhaps it is, but perhaps it is not. There is no evidence to support the claim.

Although Morocco and others have found credible evidence of hipwork and abdominal movement being used to assist with the childbirth process, that alone does not automatically mean that *raqs* originated for this purpose. It's possible that the first person to move the body in this way was a man. Or, perhaps it was a woman discovering that hip-oriented movements were useful in relieving cramps during her monthly cycle.

In any of these examples, moving the body is not sufficient, in itself, to be considered dance. "Dance," by definition, involves moving the body in a rhythmic way as a response to music. Perhaps dance came first, as a recreational activity, and women later discovered that its movements could be useful in giving birth. There is no way to know.

Origin Theory #3: Sacred Dance of Priestesses

One of the origin myths for *raqs* claims that the dance was performed by priestesses in honor of "the Goddess." This origin tale is usually not specific about which goddess, though sometimes it mentions Hathor, Isis, or Inanna.

Julia Russo Mishkin and Marta Schill open their 1973 book *The Compleat Belly Dancer* saying, "From her origins as a vital participant in pagan ritual in the days of the Pharaohs, some 3,500 years ago, the belly dance came to the United States at the turn of the twentieth century."

Jamila Salimpour, in her 1979 book, states, "Belly dancing is the term used to describe a dance which had its origins in mysticism and ritual. The ritual was accompanied by mime, whereby the priestess was the earthly representative of the Mother Goddess." This claim does not identify which goddess, which point in history, which city/temple, or which ancient writing describes it. It is a conveniently ambiguous claim, put forward as fact, with no supporting evidence.

The sacred ritual origin theory for *raqs* appears to have appeared during the rise of feminist spirituality in the 1970's. At a time when some women were rejecting patriarchal religions and looking to the divine feminine for a spiritual path, it seemed attractive to link *raqs* to women's temple rituals.

However, the available evidence does not support this theory.

In Egypt, the ancient art on the walls of temples and tombs does not actually depict someone in a position with a hip raised or pushed out in an attitude of dance.

When I hired a licensed tour guide with a degree in Egyptology for a private tour of dance-related images at the Karnak and Luxor temples, he led me to scenes of dances that consisted of leaping, walking/running, and acrobatics. The walls of these temples include handsprings similar to the one shown in the image to the right. When asked what the surrounding text on the walls said, the guide explained that it was talking about a celebration, with dance being performed as entertainment. Dance was not being used as temple ritual. He said that the priesthood was typically depicted as carrying offerings. He was not aware of any scenes in temples or tombs showing priestesses dancing to honor a goddess.

Although it is possible that some sort of ancient sacred dance existed which used hip-oriented dance technique, to date researches have not produced evidence to prove this. Even if a link to ancient priestesses could be found, that does not necessarily indicate that the dance originated in the temples – the dance could have originated elsewhere, and then later been brought into the temples.

[6] *Belly Dance: The Birth Magic Ritual*. By Jamila Salimpour. Page 3.

Origin Theory #4: Carried Westward by the Gypsies

In the mid-1990's, a new origin theory arose around *raqs*, the suggestion that it was invented in India and then carried west by the Romani during their migration. This theory appears to have been linked to people misinterpreting the motion picture *Latcho Drom*. The actual film is a travelogue, showing the different forms of music, clothing, dance, and culture in the various regions where the Romani can be found. However, some people interpreted it to be a history lesson on how cultural arts of India were carried westward and imprinted elsewhere.

A study of folk dances in the countries where the Romani have lived in large numbers shows the error of this theory. The czardas couple dance done in Hungary, for example, is quite different from the line dances seen in Romania and Bulgaria. These in turn are very different from the *raqs* found in Egypt, Turkey, and Lebanon, or the flamenco found in Spain.

It is important to consider that the Romani were not in a position of power in the places where they lived. They were often persecuted, usually relegated to the fringes of society. They lacked the social influence to replace indigenous dance forms with their own. Instead, the Romani performers learned the music and dance of the locals wherever they went, and made money as entertainers performing the locally-popular material.

Other Origin Theories

The Lebanese dancer Amani theorizes that *raqs* was invented in Iraq, then carried west via migrations. This is plausible, considering that an ancient Iraq-based civilization named Sumer is considered by some archeologists to be the oldest known civilization on earth. Amani's theory deserves further research and consideration.

Closing Thoughts

Dance scholars continue to research the history of *raqs*. As they uncover new bits of information, or apply new theories to existing evidence, it is likely that some origin theories will fall out of favor and new ones arise. However, it's unlikely facts will ever emerge proving the true origins of this dance form. Therefore, rather than continuing to search for origins, perhaps the *raqs* community would do well to consider these words from Andrea Deagon: "Sticking to fact — however little there is of it — is respectful to others, as it allows them to form their own interpretations of the dance without being influenced by 'origin myths' that might not reflect their own feelings or beliefs. But even more important, this level of caution and truthfulness is respectful of the people of the past, whose lives we do not really know and should not describe as if we did."

[7] "In Search of the Origins of Dance: Real History or Fragments of Ourselves." By Andrea Deagon. Published in *Habibi* Volume 17, Number 1 (Spring 1998), pages 35-36. Republished at http://www.shira.net/about/origins-deagon.htm, accessed February 2, 2014.

A Tribal Journey

By Carolena Nericcio-Bohlman

My dance journey began in 1974, when I walked into my first belly dance class with Masha Archer in San Francisco, CA. I was in search of movement, preferably movement that didn't require a partner. I took a belly dance class because I perceived it as a solo dance form. The irony isn't lost on me that I ultimately created a group improvisational format.

It wasn't long before I began performing with Masha Archer and the San Francisco Classic Dance Troupe. Masha's style was an eclectic blend of classic Egyptian, Folkloric, and any other influence that appealed to her. Masha, a trained painter and sculptor, taught us to create art through dance. It was this concept of art in movement rather than the specific dance technique that I carried with me to my first class as an instructor. In 1987, after the San Francisco Classic Dance Troupe disbanded, I began teaching in a small studio in the Noe Valley Ministry. My only goal was to teach people to dance so I could have dance partners.

My first students came primarily from the San Francisco underground. Being young and tattooed, I seemed to attract other young people living alternative lifestyles. Since tattoos and primitive styles of body adornment were the vogue, we began our journey into public performance at tattoo shows and conventions. Ultimately, through this underground, we became well known in San Francisco.

When the need for a name for the dance troupe arose, a friend suggested the playful rhyme FatChanceBellyDance, based on the silly question dancers often get from onlookers who think that beautiful, feminine belly dance is merely an exotic entertainment for their personal pleasure. In other words, the answer is, "Fat chance you can have a private show."

When I moved out of the San Francisco underground, into a studio, I actually saw a decline in students. In some ways, the dance was being fostered in the shadows and hidden cultures of San Francisco. Ultimately, the move to the studio allowed me to reach an audience that was not accessible previously, but I lost some of the underground vibe. Nevertheless, I gained a broader platform for the business that allowed me to ultimately grow it to where it is today.

As my troupe and I expanded horizons, we received a mixed response. Some people loved the new style; others disliked its departure from traditional Egyptian and Turkish dance styles prominent in the US at the time. Finally, the style was coined "American Tribal Style® Belly Dance," by a famous Egyptian dancer from NYC named Morocco. The intention of this label was to distance ATS® from classical beledi styles. The word "American" made it clear that ATS® was distinctly an American invention, not a traditional dance style. "Tribal Style" described the dancers working together as a group with a "tribal" look.

Back at the San Francisco studio, a system was evolving. We created basic steps inspired from

North African and Middle Eastern dance, but characterized by everyday movements. I spent a good deal of time analyzing the mechanics of movement to ensure that the beauty and simplicity of the movements flowed organically.

That focus on the organic nature of the movements coupled with the fact that our performance opportunities were largely casual, led to a dance form that was largely improvisational. There simply wasn't a way, or a need, to choreograph because the dance space often changed at the last minute, and the dancers had to perform without rehearsal or any information about the performance space. The dancers needed flexibility and the ability to communicate with one another.

Duets, trios, and quartets worked in set formations. If the stage was two-sided, or if the dance space was in the round, the dancers could flip the lead by facing the opposite direction. In other words, as long as the dancers stayed in formation, the group could face any direction and the lead could change, depending on the audience's location. I developed cues for each step or combination, usually an arm or head movement that could easily be seen. I found that because all steps began with a gesture to the right, dancers tended to angle to the left. This angle allowed following dancers to clearly see the lead dancer.

Cues and formations are the brilliance of ATS®. They are often unnoticed because of the elaborate costumes, fancy steps, exciting music, and sheer beauty of women dancing together. However, the formations and cues are the anchor of improvisational choreography. Even occasional formal choreography is created around the logic of the formations and cues.

As American Tribal Style® grew in popularity, more and more people began adapting the basics into their own vocabulary and appropriating the name. It became so confusing that I realized I needed to "take back" American Tribal Style®. I created a basic curriculum and set about touring the world teaching dancers and instructors. The General Skills training and its accompanying Teacher Training resulted. Soon, dancers all over the world were certified as "Sister Studios" agreeing to teach ATS®.

I am now spending most of my time in San Francisco, letting the FatChanceBellyDance® instructors tour the world for a while. I am working on several projects focusing on bringing dancers to San Francisco to study and learn. Staying close to home is allowing me to re-assess and plan for some exciting new chapters in the ATS® story. I have recently published a book, "American Tribal Style® Classic, Volume 1." It is a companion guide to the Classic ATS® steps presented on the DVD Volume 1. I will be following up with several other companion guides. I am collaborating on a new line of flattering clothing with Kathleen Crowley inspired by timeless designs and named after my mother, Bess. I am launching a new FCBD Studio Manager software to manage class registrations. I hope you will come along for the ride and see what the future holds.

Photographer Raymond Van Tassel. Carolena Nericcio-Bohlman **www.FCBD.com**

ALGERIAN NAILATES – THE OULED NAIL

By Halima

Ouled Nail (pronounced will-ed ni-eel) is one of the largest Berber tribes in Algeria and their name means "Children of Nail."

They are most commonly known in the western world for their dancing women. Unlike other Arab tribes who guard their daughters, the Ouled Nail mother will encourage her daughter from a young age in the art of love making and dance. Their goal is to amass a large dowry and marry as soon as possible. Once a sufficient dowry has been obtained they have no trouble finding a suitable marriage partner in their own tribe. This has been an honorable means within their tribe to insure the material well-being of themselves and their families. The men of the tribe harbor no repulsion about marrying a girl who has earned her dowry. However, once she is married she is locked up tighter than any of her tribal sisters and never dances publicly again.

Costumes until the first half of the 1900's were wonderful. They sported face tattoos, heavily kohled eyes with their oily hair worn in braids looped and held up on each side of the head by large earrings with the typical diadem sitting on top of their coiffure. When they earned enough money they purchased ostrich feathers for their tiara. They wore ruffled dresses or a loose garment called meliah, belted at the waist with fibula pins attached on each side of the dress near the collar bone. The pins held the dress or shawl in place. They were heavily adorned with gold and silver jewelry. They often wear a huge bracelet with studs and spikes an inch or more in length to protect them.

After several dances sometimes a dancer would disappear behind a screen and then return completely nude except for the headdress and jewelry to continue her performance. The women often dance in pairs. They would line up and when one dancer was tired of dancing she would be replaced so that there were always two girls dancing together. Dance movements would include shoulder shimmies, undulations, snake arms and twisting hip movements. They often used a silk scarf which flutters or is pulled behind the head or against the cheek. Arm positioning is usually held up at about shoulder level framing the upper body. Simple hand movements include delicate finger flutters. The hips move from under the waist and tilting forward or in a twisting or arch movement from side to side. The dance is usually done in two parts, the first part being the "polite" dance where they performed the more refined gliding movements. The second dance is when they return nude and display their skills learned by rotating breasts, intricate belly rolls and quivering thighs.

Shades of Andalusia

By Chellcy Mifsud-Reitsma

Chellcy and Fringe Benefits Dance Co. performing Spanish fusion in Toronto, Canada at the International Belly Dance Conference. Photo by Denise J. Marino, 2007.

Introduction

Mysterious and romantic Andalusia has a vast, complex and elusive history blanketed in a mist of speculation, fables and folklore. So too, the beautiful and passionate dances of Al-Andalus, the Romani Gypsies, and the Spanish have a vague and complexity interwoven history. There is nothing pure about the celebrated Andalusian dances, they are all the unique hybrids of illustrious and vibrant cultures that once occupied the region and were assimilated into the Spanish Andalusian culture and more recently, embraced by the Middle Eastern and North African world-wide dance community.

The ethnochoreology of Andalusia is too expansive and complex to include it all in this modest essay. Therefore, I have attempted to summarize it in a way that is palpable for dancers and dance enthusiasts to gain knowledge that is pertinent to Andalusian dance styles and deepen their appreciation and understanding of the cultures and traditions these dances stem from. How many shades of Andalusia, indeed, are embodied in the visceral journey through time that these dances animate?

In this essay I will give a brief history of Spain during the centuries that most likely hallmark the first foundations and development of Andalusian dance styles that are still being practiced today.

Starting with the Visigoths, who paved the way for the Islamic Umayyad Caliphates, and later Muslim Arabs and Berbers (all so called "Moors") to take control of most of Spain. Then I will delve into the "Moorish" occupation and decline, finishing the history section with the migration of the mysterious Romani Gypsies of India.

In the second section of the essay, the Andalusian Spanish regional dances will be introduced in short descriptions. The third section will be a historical synopsis of the passionate and intricate flamenco styles, however, the most emphases will be given to the enigmatic Zambra Mora flamenco style, as well as attempting to de-mystify it. Zambra will be highlighted since it has heavy Moorish and Gypsy influences and is the quintessence of Andalusian dance. Contemporary Flamenco and Oriental fusion will also be discussed.

Finally, the fourth section of the essay will be dedicated to depicting the soulful and elegant Andalusian Muhashahat style; developed by the infamous Mahmoud Reda of Egypt, and beautifully expanded upon and elevated by Nesma Al-Andalus of Spain.

Chellcy and Fringe Benefits Dance Co. performing Spanish fusion in Toronto, Canada at the International Belly Dance Conference. Photo by Denise J. Marino, 2007.

An Extremely Brief History of Spain: 5th -17th Centuries AD.

While reading the history section it is important to keep in mind that much of the history during these centuries was written hundreds of years after the events occurred, and the few accounts that were written during these centuries in Christian and Muslim texts, and by early historians, are extremely vague. Therefore, the history of these centuries, especially the earlier centuries, is clouded by legend and political and religious propaganda.

Visigoths

Following the decline of the Roman Empire in the 5th century AD, the Arian Christian Visigoths were one of the Germanic successors to the Western Roman Empire. Their kingdom comprised of what is today southwest France and the Iberian Peninsula. They reigned from the 5th to 8th centuries, approximately 418-720 AD.

Their entire reign is plagued with political and religious unrest, uprisings and wars. There was never ending fighting with the Suevi, Vandals, Romans, Byzantines and Franks. Still by 625 the Visigoths, with the defeat of the Byzantines, had gained control of the whole of Spain. However, they could not assimilate or make amends with the Hispania regional peoples (Basques , Asturians and Cantabrians) and passed extremely harsh laws on the Jews, which were only briefly eliminated in 654, and then reinstated in 694. So despite having absolute power over Spain, there was constant internal fighting with the locals, and civil wars over religious and political disputes for the entire Visigoth reign.

The Gothics even fought amongst themselves. One most notable of these revolts was led by the Arian bishop of Merida, against King Reccared I (586-601) son of Liuvigild; because upon his accession to the throne, Reccared I converted to Catholic Christianity causing upheaval in the Kingdom. The revolt was squelched, and the King also defeated another offensive in the North by the Franks. Then in 589, Reccared I supervised the Council of Toledo, where he denounced Arian and committed his faith to the creed of Nicene. He then took on the family name of the Constantinian dynasty, Flavius, and began fashioning himself as the successor of Roman emperors. He also had to fight the Byzantines who were gaining foothold in the south (Andalus), what was then called Hispania Baetica.

In 601 Reccared's son Liuva II became king for a very short time. He was followed by a numerous succession of Visigothic Kings, who all had short-lived reigns. During this turbulent time of power struggles between nobles and kings the church and its councils were able to gain a strong hold in religious and political power.

Near the end of the Visigothic reign, around 698, there was once again civil war, famine and disease. King Roderic, who had seized the capitol of Toledo, was at war with the sons of King Wittiza, Achila and Ardo. Then by 711 Roderic, a tyrant, was not only fighting the Basques in the North, but had also kidnapped the daughter of the nobleman Count Julian of Ceuta and raped her. According to legend, Julian was furious with Roderic and wanted to overthrow him. So he asked for help from a North African (Berber), Muslim military leader named Tariq ibn-Ziyad.

Tariq, under the orders of the Umayyad Caliph Al-Walid, led the Islamic conquest across the Straits of Gibraltar with approximately 7,000 men, while King Roderic was distracted with fighting the Basques in the north. Note: the name "**Gibraltar**" is the **Spanish** derivation of the **Arabic** name *Jabal Tāriq*, meaning "mountain of Tariq", named after him. The actual number of men Tariq entered Spain with is pure speculation and changes depending on whose history you read.

Later on July 19, Roderic died in a battle with the Umayyad's in the province of Cadiz, along the River Guadalete. It is unclear how Roderic died. The most popular theory is that, he was betrayed by his men who sided with the proper heirs to the throne (Achila and Ardo) and Julian and the Umayyad; upon which, Roderic frantically fled the battle scene and drowned in the river. The most notable contribution that the Visigoths made to Spain was the institution of the monarchy.

The "Moorish" Years:

Before beginning our journey through the remaining 8th century all the way to the 17th century, we need to understand who the main characters of this chapter are.

Who were the Umayyads?

The Umayyad (also called Omayyad), were Islamic caliphates, and a family (clan), from Mecca in Saudi Arabia. They were second in line of the Islamic Caliphates established after Muhammad's death. When Muawiya ibn Abi Sufyan, then governor of Syria, seized the caliphate, he made succession of ruler hereditary and established the Umayyad dynastic regime, and relocated the capital to Damascus in Syria. They ruled from Syria until 750, when the Abbasid revolted and took over just after the 3rd Muslim Civil War of 744-747.

Part of the Umayyad family fled Syria and lived in exile in North Africa for about six years before establishing the Umayyad Caliphate, which spanned across part of North Africa and Al-Andalus, Spain. The Umayyad Caliphate's rule ended in 750, followed by the Emirate of Cordoba until 929, then became the Caliphate of Cordoba until 1031 and the factionalized multiple independent taifa (Muslim-ruled principalities), which finally ended with the fall of the last Muslim kingdom of Granada in 1492.

Who were the Moors?

Moor is a confusing term that through the centuries has come to be an umbrella term used to identify various ethnic groups and Muslims. There are so many different and conflicting definitions of "Moor" it is mind-boggling!

From Europe to the Philippines and even Brazil the term Moor, Mouro, Moro, Moir, Mor, Moreno, Moura, Mairu, Maur, etc. has come to mean many things from describing dark skinned people, to any Muslim, to any non-Christian, un-baptized children and even enchanted fairy like creatures and supernatural mythical beings. In present day Spain "Moro" is used as a derogatory term for Moroccans specifically and sometimes any North African.

In all of my research I have come to believe that the Moors of Al-Andalus were mostly Muslim Arabs of Syria and Muslim Berbers of the Maghreb, with the Berbers out numbering the Arabs, and a small handful of other various North Africans thrown in the mix.

According to Encyclopedia Britannica:

"Moor : in English usage, a Moroccan or, formerly, a member of the Muslim population of Spain, of mixed Arab, Spanish, and Berber origins, who created the Arab Andalusian civilization and subsequently settled as refugees in North Africa between the 11th and 17th centuries. By extension (corresponding to the Spanish moro), the term occasionally denotes any Muslim in general, as in the case of the Moors of Sri Lanka (Ceylon) or of the Philippines. The word derives from the Latin Mauri, first used by the Romans to denote the inhabitants of the Roman province of Mauretania, comprising the western portion of modern Algeria and the northeastern portion of modern Morocco. Modern Mauritanians are also sometimes referred to as Moors (as with the French maure); the Islamic Republic of Mauritania, however, lies in the large Saharan area between Morocco and the republics of Senegal and Mali." **Encyclopdia Britannica**, Encyclopaedia Britannica, 1994, v.8, p.301

According to my Apple dictionary:

Moor |moŏr|noun

a member of a northwestern African Muslim people of mixed Berber and Arab descent. In the 8th century they conquered the Iberian peninsula, but were finally driven out of their last stronghold in Granada at the end of the 15th century.

DERIVATIVES

Moorish |ˈmʊrɪʃ| adjectiveORIGIN from Old French *More*, via Latin from Greek *Mauros* '*inhabitant of Mauretania.*' *Version 2.0.3 (51.5) © Copyright 2005-2007 Apple Inc., All rights reserved.*

According to Wikipedia: "The **Moors** were the **medieval Muslim** inhabitants of **Morocco**, western **Algeria**, **Western Sahara**, **Mauritania**, the **Iberian Peninsula**, **Septimania**, **Sicily** and **Malta**." "The Moors of **al-Andalus** of the **late Medieval** after the **Umayyad conquest of Hispania** in the early 8th century were initially Arabs and Berbers but later came to include people of mixed heritage, and Iberian Christian converts to Islam, known by the Arabs as *Muwalladun* or *Muladi*.[5]"

Who were the Moriscos?

After the Christian Reconquista of Spain and the final fall of the Muslim Granada emirate in 1492, many Muslims converted to Christianity in order to stay in Spain and Portugal, they were called "Moriscos". After a few Morisco revolts against the persecution and oppression of the Christian law, the Christians expelled many Muslims and Morisco from Spain in the 17th century, approximately 300,000. The majority of them relocated to parts of North Africa (Morocco, Tunisia, Lybia, and Egypt) and a few to France. Many of them joined the Barbary Corsairs and the Ottoman armies.

Still, thousands remained in Spain as many of them were native Iberians and did not speak Arabic and had never been Muslims, and some for economic reasons. Many were also able to hide by assimilating into the, then tolerated, Romani Gypsy immigrant population who were also dark skinned with similar features.

Al-Andalus (Moorish Spain)

The facts of the initial Umayyad invasion of 711 are obscured and many of the stories surrounding the invasion are steeped in legend. One possible theory is that Tariq Ibn Ziyad entered southern Spain with a small number of men, maybe 1,700, finding little resistance from the Hispania locals because they thought it was one of many short lived invasions of a trading expedition. There was a long history of North African raids into Iberia pre-dating the Islamic period. Then later in 712 they defeat King Roderic in a battle, possibly near the Guadalete River. Later, Tariq's superior Musa ibn Nusair, comes with approximately 10,000-15,000 reinforcements (mostly Berbers new to Muslim). Over the next 7 years they go on to conquer most of Hispania (including Portugal). However, they never gained control over the North where the Christian kingdoms in Asturias and the Pyrenees held strong. (Note that this theory differs from the other theory I mentioned above in the Visigothic section). In 712 the Umayyad's also conquered the Sindh and Punjab regions along the Indus River (present day Pakistan), which was one of many Muslim invasions into India that possibly initiated the migration of the Dom and Rom peoples (Gypsies) from India to the Middle East and Europe.

The Umayyad established their capital in Cordoba. Thus, Cordoba in the centuries to come became the major cultural center of Europe, the Middle East and North Africa and the foundation for the eventual European Renaissance. The Muslims brought with them education and advancements in mathematics, agriculture (including irrigation), medicine, astronomy, literature, technology, history, and much more.

In 750, back in Damascus, the Abbasid caliphs revolted against the Umayyad, taking control of the empire, executing many of the Umayyad family and moving the capital to Bagdad. Prince Abd al Rahman I escaped from the Abbasids in 750 and fled across North Africa, arriving in Spain (via the Straights of Gibraltar) 5 or 6 years later with the intent of settling in Al-Andalus. He overthrew the Abdassidian Govenor and took Cordoba. He became Emir of Cordoba and established the Umayyad Emirate or the Emirate of Cordoba, which lasted until 929. Then Abd Ar Rahman III declared the Caliphate of Cordoba, which lasted until 1031, in an effort to gain prestige and respect and unite Al-Andalus in the fight against the invasion by the Fatimids (based in Cairo, who also claimed the caliphate in opposition to the Abbasid Caliph in Baghdad).

Abd Ar Rahmas III practiced diplomacy and humaneness. He united Al-Andalus, gained control over the Christian kingdoms in the North, and stopped the Fatimids from advancing into Morocco and Al-Andalus. He also increased and strengthened diplomatic relations with Constantinople, the Berbers, France and Germany. His son, Al-Hakam, followed in his footsteps and maintained diplomacy until his death in 976. His death was the beginning of the decline of the caliphate in Spain, finally ending in 1031. These last years of the Caliphate of Cordoba were full of internal fighting and civil wars ultimately ending in the factionalism into multiple independent taifa (Muslim-ruled principalities), which finally ended with the fall of the last Muslim kingdom of Granada in 1492.

The fall of Toledo to Alfonso VI in 1085 marks the beginning of the end for the Muslim rule in Spain. In 1236 the Christians take Cordoba leaving the Emirate of Granada as the solo Muslim territory in Spain. Hundreds of years later, on 2nd of January, 1492, Emir Muhammad XII surrendered Granada to Queen Isabella I (Castille) and King Ferdinand II (Aragon) bringing Al-Andalus to an end.

The Moors and Moriscos of Granada continued to resist the Catholic oppression and religious persecution. Finally after the second revolt, 1568-1571, they were expelled from Granada and deported to other regions of Spain. Then in 1609-1614, upon perceiving the threat of an Ottoman invasion and fearing an alliance forming between the Morisco and Muslims with the Ottomans, the Spanish ordered that all Morisco and Muslims were to leave Spain. However, the Moors were so much a part of Spain now is was impossible to completely eradicate them. Some villages were entirely Morisco and Muslim, as was much of the work force, and there were also native Iberians who had converted to Muslim during their occupation. Furthermore, some Spanish found it un-ethical to force the Morisco who were born and raised always as Christians (not converts) out of their home, which was Spain. It was also problematic to expel the Morisco parents of Christian born children from Spain leaving thousands of children orphaned. Therefore, many Morisco and Muslims remained in Spain.

The Different Periods of Moorish Rule 711 to 1492 AD

The Dependent Emirate (711 to 756 AD) or Umayyad Caliphate:

Umayyads of Damascus till 750, Abbisid of Baghdad 750-756

The Independent Emirate (756 to 929 AD) or Umayyad Emirate or Emirate of

Cordoba or Emir of Cordoba

The Caliphate (929 to 1031 AD) or Caliphate of Cordoba

The Almoravid Era (1031 to 1130 AD) Berber dynasty of Morocco aided Al-Andalus'

Taifa Princes in staving off the inevitable Christian Reconquista.

Decline of the Muslims (1085 to 1492 AD)

Al-Andalus is hailed as the **"Golden Age"** of Spain. The Arabs brought with them the pursuit of knowledge and education to Europe. Cordoba became an intellectual center. Most advances occurred under the Caliphate. They introduced paper to the West and built one of the largest libraries in the world containing more than 400,000 texts, including translations of ancient Greek texts (in Latin, Arabic, and Hebrew). During the Caliphate the advancements in science, philosophy, medicine, music, language, poetry, geography, architecture, astronomy, history, and agriculture were prolific. In addition, they introduced new crops to Spain (like cotton, eggplants, pomegranates, hard wheat and more) and revitalized many industries. In fact, much of what is considered to be the "real Spain" has been passed down from Moors of Al-Andalus.

While most of Europe was experiencing one of the darkest periods in history, the Medieval period or Middle Ages (5th-15th centuries), Al-Andalus was becoming the pinnacle of civilization. Historian James Burke stated it best when describing the 9th century "At a time when London was a tiny mud-hut village that could not boast of a single street lamp, in Córdoba there were half a million inhabitants, living in 113,000 houses. There were 700 mosques and 300 public baths spread throughout the city. The streets were paved and lit. The houses had marble balconies for summer and hot-air ducts under the mosaic floors for winter. They were adorned with gardens with artificial fountains and orchards. Paper, a material still unknown to the west, was everywhere. There were bookshops and more than seventy libraries."

In addition to establishing an abundant amount of libraries, they opened many schools, universities and bookstores. People came from all over Europe, North African and the Middle East to study in Al-Andalus, especially Cordoba. The translated ancient texts and philosophy and the medieval Muslim and Jewish works that European scholars brought back with them to their own countries spurred the early Renaissance of the 12th century in Western Europe and set the stage for the Italian Renaissance (14th-16th centuries) and later the scientific revolution (16th-18th centuries). The legacy of Moorish Spain was consequential to the advancement of Europe and Western civilization.

Gitanos of Spain (Romani Gypsies)

The mysterious Gitanos of Spain have uncertain origins, and no oral or written history. Based on linguistic and genetic studies it is widely accepted that the Gitanos (Kales of Iberia), like all gypsies around the world are descendants of the diasporic ethnic group of Romani (Rom, Roma, Romany, Romanies, Romanis or Romane collectively) and possibly Domari originally from India. They are called many names around the world and are considered to be sub-groups like Kale, Calé, Sinti, Romanichal, Bashalde, Lovari, Luri, Curari, Xoraxai, Boyash, and many more. Each sub-group speaks different, yet similar dialects of the Indo-Aryan language of Romani often mixed with the regional language where they are living, becoming a Para-Romani language. Some sub-groups do not ascribe the term Romani or Rom to identify their ethnicity; rather they use the sub-group name, but may claim to speak Romani. Many Gypsies are fluent in the language of the country in which they are living; such as most Gitano in Spain speak Caló, which is several dialects of Spanish mixed with Romani, as well as fluent Spanish.

The terms "Gitano" (Spanish) and "Gypsy" (English) possibly derived from the words "Egyptiano" and "Egyptian" in medieval times due to the misconception that the Romani came from Egypt. The exact migration routes of the Romani and Domari are unknown, however, it is of popular belief that they first went through the Middle East, then some went on to North Africa, while others went through Greece and Eastern Europe. It is believed that the Gitano entered Spain from both the south via North Africa, and from the north via France.

The Romani and Domari of India are believed to have left India around the 6th century due to Islamic expansion and in particular raids by Mahmud of Ghazni.

They may have migrated in several waves over a period of centuries, the Dom and Rom in separate migrations. They possibly originated in the area that is now Rajasthan and migrated to the Sindh, Punjab and Baluchistan regions along the Indus River (in present day Pakistan). The Rom and Dom possibly share similar origins but their languages are distinctly different, even though they share many similarities. Both languages are relative to the present day Hindustani languages spoken in Northern India and Pakistan.

There are few historical records regarding the Romani, and due to their dark skin and style of clothing, many were confused with Egyptians or Muslims (could be from any country). The first record of Romani in Europe was a recorded slave trade transaction in Wallachia (present day Romania) in 1385. However, the Romani had most likely been in Europe for centuries already. The first record known in existence documenting the Romani arrival in Spain dates back to 1425 in Zaragoza.

Chellcy performing in Florida. Photo by Denise J. Marino 2007

Though, initially the Rom and Dom were of the Hindu faith, most Gypsies adopted the religion of the country in which they were living, either by forced assimilation, laws of the land, missionaries reached them, or to escape persecution. Yet, most Gypsies still retained some of their Hindu customs, beliefs and practices.

In 1492, King Ferdinand and Queen Isabella finally had total control of Spain. They began a cultural cleansing and passed harsh laws against the Jews and Muslims, despite being Christians, the Romani were included in the persecution. All "non-Christians" were forced to assimilate or leave Spain. They passed laws to ban Gypsy style clothing, forbade them to marry within the Gypsy ethnic community, prohibited the use of the Romani language, banned their rituals, prohibited them from traveling in groups, and much more. This persecution lasted in many forms until the death of General Francisco Franco in 1975.

Traditionally occupations of the Gitanos were horse traders, dancers, musicians, blacksmiths, and fortune-tellers. This may partially be due to the fact that they were prohibited to work in most other sectors of society and forced to live in the lowest rungs of Spanish society greatly limiting their choice of occupations.

Never the less flamenco music and dance became an outlet for the gypsies to express themselves and through the soulful, deep cante jondo (hondo = deep) in particular the Gitano could reflect on and share their hardships with the world. Flamenco song and dance became synonymous with Gitano, so much so, that throughout certain periods in history particular styles of flamenco song, dance, and costume were outlawed, in particular the styles with a "Moorish" influence like the "Zambra Mora". However, persecution was not always limited to the Gypsies, Moors and Jews, under the dictatorship of the Francisco Fanco Regime (1939-1975) all things regional were banned. Franco believed that to create a unified and homogenized Spain, Regional "separatism" must be eradicated. He turned Spain upside down and inside out hunting down separatists. Howeve extensive and far reaching his efforts were, he never succeeded in completely annihilating regional dialects, customs, culture, pride, history, music and folk arts.

Eminent Dances of Andalusia

Upon researching the enigmatic history of Spain and the myriad of inhabitants over the centuries, one can ascertain that many aspects of the Spanish society, culture, and generally most things regarded as Spanish or the "real Spain" stem from a culmination of cultures. This unique hybridization is manifest in every fiber of Andalusia and is epitomized in Andalusian culture, language, people, architecture, dance, music, poetry and more. Flamenco music and dance are the jewels of this hybridization and the Gitano are the channels of communication, expression, and preservation fostering the sustainability and advancement of this multi-cultural legacy.

There are three major groupings of Spanish dances Regional (folkloric), Classical (Escuela Bolera or Spanish ballet), and Flamenco. As well, there are sub-groupings: Neo-Classical, Neo Flamenco, and Contemporary. The Regional dances can be further categorized as court dances and religious or ritual dances. Regarding some dances, especially in the South, the line between what is regional and what is flamenco is extremely blurry, and not everyone agrees. For example, in my research I found that the styles of Sevillanas and Zambra are considered by some flamenco, and regional by others. In my personal opinion many styles originate as a regional dance and then are slowly assimilated into flamenco and eventually gain national and even international recognition thereby launching them into the flamenco canon. When one considers that Castanets are mostly performed in the regional styles and in the classical styles; they are not traditionally part of flamenco dance, one can see how regional styles were appropriated into flamenco. As well, flamenco itself could even be considered a regional dance since it originated in the region of Andalusia.

A few important Spanish dance terms defined that might appear in this essay:

BAILE – dance, also called danza
CAJON – flamenco drum, rhythm box
CANTE CHICO - light happy songs and dances (small or little)
CANTE JONDO – serious and heavier songs and dances (jondo = deep)
CASTANUELAS –castanets, wooden or fiber glass shell like cymbals, tied to the thumbs
COMPAS – rhythms or bars of music, rhythmic measure of time
CONTRA TIEMPO – counter rhythm (counter time)
COPLA – verse in song
ENTRADA – entrance made by the dancer
ESTRIBILLOS – refrains, or short verses, ending
FLOREO – hand movements, flourishes
GOLPE – beat
JALEO – shouts of encouragement
LLAMADA – a call through dance or music to signal the beginning or end of a section
MANTON – large shawl
OLE - bravo
PALMAS – stylized hand claps
PASO DOBLE – double step
TIEMPOS – time of music
TOQUE – guitar playing
VUELTA – turning step
ZAPATEADO – rhythmic beats of heels and ball of foot

Spanish Regional Dances

The origins of the plentiful regional dances of Spain are quite vague and complicated and warrant an entire book on their own. However, there are a few of the dances with clear origins and many of the regional dances have a common thread. The most consistent commonality is the music and instruments. It is important to note that folkloric dances around the world tend to have more simple steps, and simple arm placements. In any country, these dances are primarily social dances, the dances of the people and were not originally intended as staged entertainment. In the Spanish folkloric dances the most notable differences are that in the north, especially the Basque region, they are chico (little), lighter and quicker paced and the music has a noticeably Celtic influence. While in the south, the dances and music are more grounded and jondo (deep), with noticeable Moorish and Gypsy influences. Throughout the myriad of dances one thing remains at the heart of all Spanish dance, rhythm (compás). I will focus this section on the regional dances of Andalusia and especially those dances with a clear Oriental influence. However, it is important to note some characteristics of the other regional styles in order to make evident the distinctive attributes of the Andalusian styles.

The northern regions of Spain and the islands have a plethora of folkloric and ritual dances. Each region, and sometimes each village, has numerous folk dances that are performed in different social gatherings, festivals, and ceremonies. The Basque region (Vascongodas), in particular, has an innumerable variety of dances.

The music of the Northern dances is typically made up of these instruments: Trikitrixa (type of accordion), guitar, castanets, triangle, guitarró (small four-stringed guitar), bandúrria (plucked stringed instrument related to the lute), violin, xeremies (bagpipes), flabiol (small wooden flute), and the ximbomba (friction drum) and the tambuorine. In the South there are a wider variety of wind instruments played including reed instruments, as well the lute and its many variations, a large frame drum with cymbals on it (similar to a tambourine but larger), the guitar, the rebec (early ancestor of the violin), bass drum, violin, castanets (castañuelas), darbouka (tabla or goblet drum) and the tamborine. The instruments of both the north and the south have evolved and changed over the centuries. Today the guitar has come to dominate all Spanish music.

In the south of Spain, the region of Andalusia boasts one of the most copious histories of folkloric dance and music. Heavily influenced by the Moors, a few of the dances of the south include: Sevillanas, reminiscent of flamenco, it is a joyful and undeniably happy style. The zambra started as a Moorish dance, and was conserved by the Moors during the Reconquest by adapting it to traditional Spanish music and dance trends. As I stated before the sevillanas and the zambra can be considered both regional and flamenco. However, since the sevillana is traditionally performed with castanets and originates in Sevilla I will include it in the regional dances for the purposes of this essay. According to the Spanish Dance Society at Trinity College London, where I am studying to obtain my levels in flamenco dance, Zambra is a flamenco dance and rhythm and Sevillanas is a regional dance. Other dances native to Andalusia are the many variations of fandango, considered to be a Gypsy and Iberian mix they utilize a pattern of alternating coplas and estribillos. Two most popular versions of fandango come from Malaga and are the Verdiales and Malaguenas. Although originally regional, both have also been incorporated into flamenco, the latter of which has classical versions as well. Truly it is difficult to categorize many of the Spanish dances or define their origins due to the centuries cross cultural sharing and blending of dance and music styles.

Comprehensively, the regional dances of Spain are essentially European and Arabic in composition yet simultaneously, uniquely Spanish in origin. Two of the most popular regional dance styles are the Jota and the Fandango. Each region has their own distinct versions of the Jota and Fandango, signified by the musical instruments and the costuming of the dancers, as well as the stylization of the movements. In each style the castanets are sometimes played. In the south of Spain the Jota has a heavier, sober quality with quick, sharp steps, and heel stamps; with the hands held high, mostly overhead and sometimes the dancers play castanets. The jota most likely originated in the region of Aragon in the north, but spread throughout Spain. The jota can have a 3/4 or 6/8 rhythm with a waltz like feeling to the steps. However, there is a legend that Aben Jot, a Moorish poet of Andalusia, was exiled in the north and brought the jota with him. The jota music precedes the dance and the verses are improvised.

The Fandango is lighter and faster paced than the Jota and is usually triple metre. Its origins are unclear but variations of fandango now exist in most regions of Spain. It may have origins in South America or in the Indies and some argue that it stemmed from the jota, regardless it is most commonly linked to Andalusian culture now-a-days and is its own distinct regional style. The dance is traditionally performed in couples and is accompanied with castanets or palmas (hand-clapping). The timing was originally in a 6/8 rhythm and eventually in 3/4 and 3/8.

Malaga in the south of the Andalusian region, boasts many styles of fandango, however there are five styles in particular that are essential to fandango: the Verdiales, Malaguenas, Abandolaos, Jaberas and Rondenas. Most notably the Verdiales comes from the mountains near Malaga; the term refers to the green olives grown in the area. This dance was traditionally a celebratory dance performed at an annual festival called Fiesta Major de Verdiales, on the feast day of Santos Innocentes. It is believed that all the other fandango styles in Malaga derived from the Verdiales. The Verdiales has a three-count pattern with strong emphasis given to the second beat.

The costuming for the folkloric dances varies from region to region. However there are a few commonalities. For example, most of the regional dances are performed in rope-soled shoes called alpargatas or shoes that lace up the ankle, white stockings are worn by both men and women, colorful ribbons are tied to the thumb or middle finger when castanets are being played, and many of the men's costumes have sashes tied around the waist, while the women often wear skirts and a bodice or apron.

The Sevillianas is probably the most popular of all the Spanish regional dances and the most difficult. It requires full body and mind coordination utilizing the hands, feet, arms, facial expressions and castanet playing and zapateado (stamping rhythms with the feet). It is a type of folk music and dance from Seville in Andalusia, which is now taught in dance schools around the world. It can be considered a bridge between the regional and flamenco dances. Some consider the sevillanas the "true flamenco" while others consider it to be a regional dance, and still others regard it as its own independent dance. A sevillana is a four-part music with an accompanying four-part dance and usually danced in partners, but can also be performed in a group. It symbolizes the four stages of courtship. The time signature is 3/4 and sometimes 6/8, it belongs to the seguidillas family. The most important elements of sevillanas music are the guitar and the singer, as well as the clapping and/or castanets. The music may also include other traditional Spanish instruments. It should also be noted that there is a particular style of sevillana, the sevillanas boleras that is danced by the Escuela Bolera.

Flamenco

Flamenco, declared by UNESCO as a "Masterpiece of the Oral and Intangible Heritage of Humanity" in 2010, has become a worldwide celebrated and academically studied dance and music form. Originating in Andalusia, flamenco has forevermore been considered the artistic outlet of the poor and oppressed. It is a folk art passed on through the generations by oral tradition. Often the styles are particular to a family, where upon each individual artist is encouraged to use the tradition as a foundation for building their own unique style of self-expression.

Flamenco is a hybrid dance and music which most certainly is comprised of musical and dance influences from all the peoples that once inhabited Spain through the centuries, with the strongest elements stemming from indigenous Andalusians, Moors, Jews, and Indians. Many dance ethnologists point out the similarities between flamenco and the Kathak of India. Both have similar hand movements with circling and fanning the fingers, as well the zapateado is similar to the footwork found in Kathak. Thanks to their oral traditions and itinerancy, Gitanos can be credited with the preservation, many innovations and spreading of the flamenco arts throughout the world. Today, and for centuries, flamenco is considered to be a tripartite art incorporating dance, singing, and the guitar simultaneously. As well, rhythmic accents through palmas, zapateado, castanets and the cajon are integral to the flamenco arts.

Chellcy (center) performing flamenco with the Paul Curmi Dance Co. in Malta. Directed by Eldridge Saliba-Curmi (right). Photo by Leonard Cocks 2013.

The first foundations of flamenco possibly date back to the 16th century, originally performed in private settings and parties or celebrations. It was only in the 19th century that flamenco became publicly performed as staged entertainment. Major developments occurred during the "Golden Age of Flamenco" (1869-1910), when the café cantante reigned supreme on the scene (the first café cantante opened in Sevilla in 1842). The 19th century saw a rise of international popularity in flamenco and the Gitana. Then 1892-1956 marks the "Theatrical" period or the "Opera Flamenco" period in which flamenco was brought to the big stage and commercialized. During this period a new genre developed, Andalusian Couplet (Copla Andaluza), an orchestral fusion of Andalusian folk, flamenco, and zarzuela (an operatic and orchestral style with two main periods, Baroque and Romantic).

There are innumerable genres within flamenco, which fall under umbrella terms such as alegrias, bulerias, fandangos, malaguenas, rondena, seguiriyas, soleares, tientos, and more. But according to musician Paco Pena, there are four fundamental styles in Flamenco: Soleares, Bulerias, Tientos, and Seguirillas, all the other styles just further serve to categorize the numerous flamenco variations. Each style is defined by tones, melodies, rhythms, and harmonic structures

~ 38 ~

attributed to each style and their regional variations. Some theorize that primitive flamenco consisted of just singing, palmas and finger snapping, while others claim that there were also styles, which were indeed accompanied by music. Regardless, the most important element of flamenco is the singer. Hadia (well known Oriental dancer of Canada) describes the influences on the evolution of flamenco singing and music in a very clear way in her essay *Spanish Gypsy and Flamenco Dance History:*

The strongest influences evident in the evolution of Flamenco singing and music can be traced from:
Punjabi singing of India
Persian Zyriab song form
Classical Andalusian Orchestras of the Islamic Empire
Jewish Synagogue Chants
Mozarabic forms such as Zarchyas and Zambra
Arabic Zayal which themselves are the foundation for Fandangos
Andalusian regional folk forms
Western African influences via the slaves of the New World Caribbean, Central and South American colonies. These include Rumba, Garotin, Guajiras, Columbianas, etc. (Hadia, *Spanish Gypsy and Flamenco Dance History*, Centralhome.com Company Inc.)

The café cantantes were influential in the development of flamenco as we know it today. Around 1915 there was a decline in the popularity of the café cantates due to the increasing popularity of the Opera Flamenco. In 1922, Federico Garcia Lorca and Manuel de Falla led a team of artists and intellectuals in organizing the Concurso del Cante Jondo, a festival and singing contest, held in Granada at the Alhambra. Lorca had a deep passion and love for all things Spanish folk. He was alarmed by the commercialism he saw in the Opera, and by the rapidly vanishing flamenco and folk styles and traditions. According to Lorca, "The artistic treasure of an entire race is passing into oblivion." He sought to re-popularize authentic flamenco and the café cantantes. In the 1930's Lorca joined forces with the dancer and choreographer, La Argentinita. 1931 was a busy year for Lorca; he published his book Poema del Cante Jondo a tribute to café cantante performances and released to the public recordings of popular, old, Spanish songs widely performed in the café cantante era, recorded with La Argentinita.

The Contemporary flamenco era began in the 1930's with the development of the tablao flamenco, later the cuadro flamenco, created by Federico Garcia Lorca and La Argentinita. Tablao flamenco is, "a contemporary nightclub where flamenco is performed on a raised wooden stage, the term derived from the word tablado, which refers to a wooden board or plank, or a wooden planked stage. In contemporary flamenco, the terms tablao flamenco and cuadro flamenco often refer to the same event. Dances performed in a cuadro or tablao flamenco can be completely choreographed, totally improvised, or generally, include a combination of both these characteristics and are structured improvisations." (Katherine Thomas, aka Katerina Tomás, 1994)

Reminiscent of café cantantes, La Argentinita, created the Café de Chinítas, which is choreographically based on the cuadro flamenco (a traditional flamenco performing ensemble, can also include regional dances). It was performed "throughout the United States, Europe and South America from the late 1930s until 1945. La Argentinita's Café de Chinítas contributed significantly to the internationalization of the cuadro flamenco form. Thus, the traditional, contemporary cuadro flamenco takes its structure from the café cantante period." (Katherine Thomas, aka Katerina Tomás, 1994, from *Theatrical Flamenco Dance and Music Legacy of Federico García Lorca and La Argentinita*)

In his essay focused on flamenco guitar, *History of Flamenco,* Francois Faucher created a table categorizing the flamenco styles as such:

Flamenco: form/family/style

Gypsy (cante Gitano)
Soleares family:
　　　　Soleares, La Cana, Alegrieas, Bulerias
Seguiriya family:
　　　　Seguiriyas, Serranas
Tientos family:
　　　　Tientos, Zambras, Tangos, Tanguillos
Andalusian (cante andaluz):
Fandangos family:
　　　　Fandangos grandes
　　　　Fandangos de Huelva
　　　　Granadinas (Granainas)
　　　　Media Granainas
　　　　Malaguenas
　　　　Verdiales
　　　　Minera
　　　　Rondena
　　　　Tarantas
　　　　Tarantos
Folk-influenced:
Farruca
Garrotin
Petenera
Sevillanas
Villancico
El Vito
Latin American-Influenced:
Guajiras
Colombianas
Rumba

Zambra

Zambra or Zambra Mora (also called Danza Arabe and Danza Mora) is a flamenco style that has all but vanished into extinction. It is a much disputed style, some don't believe in its existence and believe it to be a fantasy dance invented by belly dancers, some think it is a regional dance, and others categorize it as a style of flamenco stemming from the tientos style. Obviously, the history and origins of zambra are extremely un-clear and un-certain. In all of my research, dance studies, and visits to Andalusia I have deducted that Zambra Mora does exist, and is a form of flamenco with Moorish roots and was assimilated into the Gitano culture where it was further developed.

Amaya, creator of the award winning "Gypsy Fire" Documentary. Photo by Andre Elbing

Luckily a few artists today are working hard to keep the zambra alive, Puela Lunaris of Spain currently living in New York, and Amaya of New Mexico are two of them. Both of these artists have written about zambra and produced educational videos and documentaries about zambra, they are great resources for dancers to broaden and deepen their understanding of Zambra. Amaya's award winning *Gypsy Fire* documentary is very informative and entertaining, and includes footage of the dancers of the Sacromonte, historical dancers, interviews and some dance instruction at the end in zambra. Puela Lunaris has been hailed by the New York City Center Education Department as a "World-renowned teacher, researcher and dancer, who carries the flame of an almost forgotten ancient Flamenco Tradition, **The Zambra Flamenca**," She claims Zambra as part of her cultural heritage and has spent two decades researching, rescuing and teaching the zambra tradition. She also has an informative instructional DVD *Zambra Flamenca*, which includes the history of zambra and teaches a flamenco chorography.

***Puela Lunaris performing Zambra at the Theatrical Belly Dance
Conference in New York City. Unknown photographer, 2010.***

 As well, Ana Ruiz wrote a wonderfully informative book called Vibrant Andalusia in which she dedicated an entire chapter solely to zambra. She states: "Zambra Mora is not and never was a dance, it is a form of Flamenco song and guitar with the most heaviest Middle Eastern influence of all the 'palos' or styles of Flamenco music." However, according to the Spanish Dance Society of Trinity College, London, zambra is Moorish music, song, dance, and poetry and a style of flamenco. Zambra was deemed the "Forbidden Dance" and outlawed at various points in history after the Reconquista. It is also a three-part wedding dance that represents the phases of Gitano weddings particular to the Sacromonte. In his book Teoria Del Cante Jondo, Hipolito Rossy claims that there are historical references to a dance called zambra that date back to the 15th century, and that by the 17th century it ranked alongside popular dances like fandangos, zapateado, and zarabanda. He goes on further to claim that zambra was originally a lively Moorish dance.

The term zambra may come from the Arabic word samira meaning: evening companion with lively conversation or an all-night party, or more likely from Maghrebi Arabic (Morocco) zambra, meaning: party. Zambra Mora means Moorish party or celebration. According to Puela Lunaris zambra is a binary rhythm sometimes written as a 2/4 or a 4/4. The Spanish Dance Society also concurs and adds that it is most similar to tangos in compas, but uses a different chord structure. My flamenco instructor and dance partner in Malta, Eldridge Saliba-Curmi, likened the zambra rhythm to farucca, only slower. It is interesting to point out that both tango and zambra stem from the tientos family and that farucca comes from the folk influenced flamenco styles. It is widely believed that zambra traditionally is performed barefoot, with small finger cymbals (crotalos, similar to Turkish zils and Egyptian sagat), or sometimes a tambourine, and has more freedom in the hips and a lot of circling hands and arms demonstrating its strong Moorish influences and lively and chico with a lot of jaleo. Some say that the zambra costuming was a top tied at the ribs with a bare midriff, a skirt low on the hips with a ruffle at the bottom, and a hip-scarf. However, I think that this is highly unlikely considering that the dance may have originated from the Moors who were Muslim and further developed in later centuries that were markedly oppressive due to persecution by conservative Catholic's.

Another theory on the origins of zambra defines it as an all-night, open-air party with music, cante, poetry, and feasting held in the summer in Seville after the fall of Cordoba. Originally artists and intellectuals of Moorish, Jewish and Christian faiths presented their latest works at the zambra. All the theories on the origins, original movements, and even the costuming of the enigmatic zambra are just that, "theories" and some may be based on facts. No matter, zambra is undoubtedly the most Moorish of all the flamenco styles. According to Paco Pena, "Zambra Mora is a Moorish dance which demonstrates the strongest of these influences. Its unmistakable character is partly created by returning the sixth string of the guitar to D."

*Puela Lunaris **teaching Zambra at the Spring Caravan/Rakkasah Festival.
Photo by Bruce Bishop, 2013.***

Because zambra is a somewhat confusing term applied to dance, music, parties, poetry, rhythm etc., it has been said that zambra is still performed by the Gypsies in the caves of the Sacromonte, above Granada. However, when I visited the Rocio Cave in the Sacromonte what I saw was a type of flamenco dance performed in flamenco shoes, not barefoot, with zapateado and no finger cymbals. There was a heavier, sexier, raw feeling to the music, cante, and dance, as well as more hip movements than other flamenco performances I have witnessed. I also observed the dancers back stage (in a side room of the main hall of the cave) full on belly dancing in between sets just for fun! Because I displayed a lot of enthusiasm throughout the evening, near the end of the show one of the dancers asked me to join her on stage. I was very excited and it was a lot of fun. After the show the Rocio Cave show manager and guitarist asked me how long I was staying in Granada and if I would like to make "flamenco belly dance" shows for the tourists at the Alhambra. I was really honored but had to decline since I was only staying there for a few days on holiday break in the middle of my teaching and performance tour. According to Ana Ruiz the flamenco I saw in the Rocio Cave is a "type of Flamenco strongly inspired by the Moors called Zambra Por Moro that has a pulsating, somber, dramatic feel." Eldridge Saliba-Curmi told me that zambra is flamenco but should not include stamping and should be performed barefoot. He said the movements are slow and sensual, including a lot of circling hands and arms and has a sexy and serious attitude. Regardless, what I witnessed in the Rocio Cave was certainly different than any other flamenco performance I've seen in Sevilla, Madrid, Barcelona, or in Malta and the USA.

Fusions Inspired by Andalusia

Rakkasah West instructors Chellcy and Eldridge, performing as their ChelEl duet (theatrical flamenco Oriental fusion). Photo by Carl Sermon, 2013.

Dance, like life is ever changing, it is a living, growing, evolving art. Artists are always making new fusions and innovations. I believe that all artists should have a strong foundation in the dance traditions that they choose to fuse, creating educated fusion, not confusion. In recent years new fusion styles are emerging on the Oriental dance scene. These fusions consist of flamenco and regional Spanish dance styles fused with a myriad of dances: Oriental (Egyptian and Turkish styles), Latin dances, Indian dances, hip-hop, Tribal (Tribal fusion, stemmed from American Tribal Style), and more. One can also interpret these dances as fusions inspired by or incorporating a Spanish dance influence.

Nesma and Rafael Jimemez performing flamenco Oriental fusion.
Photo by Erik Godfroid.

There have been many names given to these fusions, for example: Oriental Flamenco, Flamenco Oriental, Tribal Flamenco, Zingari, Gypsy Fusion, Spanish Fusion, Andalusian Fusion, Dark Gypsy, Danza Arabe and mistakenly Zambra or Zambra Mora. A few examples of contemporary artists in the belly dance scene that I feel have created strong, reputable fusions are Mahmoud Reda of Egypt, Nesma Al Andalus of Spain, Rafael Jimenez of Spain, Mares of Spain, Amaya of USA, Puela Lunaris of USA, Amira of Las Vegas, Eldridge Saliba-Curmi of Malta, and Chellcy Mifsud-Reitsma of Malta and USA (myself). When artists create fusion responsibly and can root it in a historical context it can result in a beautiful and unique style worthy of carrying on for generations. One example of this is Muhashahat.

Amira and Chellcy performing an Andalusian inspired Spanish fusion piece at Rakkasah West.
Photo by Carl Sermon, 2012.

Muhashahat

Nesma and her Al-Andalus Dance Co. performing Muhashahat. Photo by Eric Godfroid

The soulful and elegant Andalusian Muhashahat (Muwashahaat) dance style (also called Arabo-Andalusi); developed by the infamous Mahmoud Reda of Egypt, and beautifully expanded upon and elevated by Nesma Al-Andalus of Spain, is a tribute to the Al-Andalus era. Inspired by the muhashahat music, Reda created 8 famous muhashahats (also spelled moxahats) in 1979. This style was inspired by Reda's vision of what court dancing may have resembled in Al-Andalus. To create the movements he borrowed from Southern European folk dances and fused it with his own unique Reda style of Oriental.

Mahmoud Reda with Nesma. Photo by Eric Godfroid.

The Muhashahat music comes from the classical Arabic poetry of the Al-Andalus era and was set to music composed in the 18th -20th centuries. The muwashahat style is performed to primarily three rhythms. One of my instructors and mentors, musician and dancer Karim Nagi documented these rhythms as follows:

YORK SAMAI 6/8 (for Muwashahaat and Dervish)
Count: 1 2 3 4 5 6
Sound per count: D T T D T is

SAMAI THAQIL
Count: 1 2 3 4 5 6 7 8 9 10
Sound per count: D is is T is D D T is is

ANDALUSI MUHAGGAR 14/4   (for Muwashahaat)
1 2 3 4 5 6 7 8 9 10 11 12 13 14
D D D is T is D -   T is T T is T T

Another great resource for better understanding medieval music from the Middle East during the same centuries as the Al-Andalus era of Spain is professor Dr. George Sawa's book <u>Music Performance Practice in the Early Abbasid Era</u>. In his research on medieval music he found that the rhythms commonly used were: 6/8, 3/4, 3/2, 4/4, 4/2, 5/4, and 5/2 and the songs had a very complex tonal system. So possibly the Samai Thaqil and Andalusi Muhaggar developed later.

Moxahat lyrics are a poetical form born in Al-Andalus but spread through many Arabic countries and became widely popular in the Arab world. There is a famous Andalusian inspired love song, which has been mistakenly hailed by many as an authentic Andalusian song, the Lamma Bada Yatathanna. This song is not from the Al-Andalus era; rather it is from the 19th century. Some believe the music was composed by Egyptian composer, Selim Al Masri and the poetry source is unknown. Others believe it is a 19th century Ottoman piece and the lyrics are imitating the Andalusian muwashahat style. Nesma of Spain stated that this song is "not Spanish music, nor ancient music from Al-Andalus." It has "what we call "Andalusian Stetic" but not really original from Spain or Al-Andalus times." The Lamma Bada Yatathanna is written is a strange, old dialect of Arabic that is difficult to translate so there are many different translations. I've included three different translations below:

Translation is by Chris Vancil:
When she started to walk with a swinging gait
Her beauty amazed me

I have become prisoner of her eyes
Her stem folded as she bent

O my promise, O my perplexity
Who can answer my complaint
About love and suffering
But the beautiful one?

The translation listed in Hamza EL Din's album
Eclipse:
When the gossamer nymph appears,
My beloved's beauty drives me to distraction;
Surrender
Surrender
When I am enraptured by a glimpse,
My beloved's beauty is a tender branch caught by the breeze;
Surrender
Surrender
Oh my destiny, my perplexity,
No one can comfort me in my misery,
In my lamenting and suffering for love,
But for the one in the beautiful mirage;
My beloved's beauty drives me to distraction,
Surrender
Surrender

Translation by Mimi Spencer & M. Metal:
When he (she) appeared, undulating, ah! Mercy!
My love's beauty charmed us.

With a look, a wink, the lover captivated us;
When the branch swayed gracefully, we were devastated.

My promise - O my puzzlement!
Who can sympathize with my complaint of love,
Except the King of beauty?

Nesma performing her Andalusi Style. Photo by Eric Godfroid.

Nesma of Spain is the artistic director of Al-Andalus Dance Company and one of the protégés of Mahmoud Reda. Nesma lived, studied, and performed in Egypt for years under the guidance of

Reda. She learned many styles of dance from Reda but fell passionately in love with the muwashahat. This dance is what inspires her the most. In my interview of Nesma she stated, "Reda inspired me to create my new Andalusian style and taught me a lot in dance and in life." Upon returning from Egypt to Spain in 1998, Nesma founded her dance company Al-Andalus. She has since become one of the most influential forerunners of muwashahat. She has made innovations in the dance style by adding her own Oriental dance style, and elements of Egyptian and Spanish folklore. She has had great success in elevating this dance style and even premiered her show "Dreams of Al-Andalus" in 2008 at the Cairo Opera House and the Alexandria Opera House and opened for the International festival of Music In Citadel of Cairo for the Minister of Culture. Nesma believes that she accomplished this because of her new Andalusian dance style, conservative costumes and musical production. This was a near impossible feat considering that Oriental dance is of such ill repute in conservative, Muslim Egypt. Today Nesma is a world-renowned pioneer in Andalusian dance and flamenco Oriental fusions. She produces all of the music she dances to in Cairo, bringing with her the poetic forms from Al Andalus.

The Arab influence and the mysterious lure of all things Oriental has certainly had a far reaching impact on many cultures, art, literature, music and dance through the centuries and continues to inspire to this day. I leave you with a poem by Walter de la Mare, which inspired me throughout writing this essay, *Shades of Andalusia.*

Arabia by Walter de la Mare
Far are the shades of Arabia,
Where the Princes ride at noon,
'Mid the verdurous vales and thickets,
Under the ghost of the moon;
And so dark is that vaulted purple
Flowers in the forest rise
And toss into blossom 'gainst the phantom stars
Pale in the noonday skies.

Sweet is the music of Arabia
In my heart, when out of dreams
I still in the thin clear mirk of dawn
Descry her gliding streams;
Hear her strange lutes on the green banks
Ring loud with the grief and delight
Of the dim-silked, dark-haired Musicians
In the brooding silence of night.

They haunt me -- her lutes and her forests;
No beauty on earth I see
But shadowed with that dream recalls
Her loveliness to me:
Still eyes look coldly upon me,

Nesma performing her Andalusi.

Photo by Eric Godfroid

Cold voices whisper and say --
'He is crazed with the spell of far Arabia,
They have stolen his wits away.'

About the Author: Chellcy Mifsud-Reitsma

Internationally renowned, cultural dance artist; Chellcy has performed and taught workshops all over Europe, Canada, and the U.S. and is the artistic director and choreographer for **Fringe Benefits International Dance Company** in Chicago, U.S.A. and Malta, E.U. She is a highly sought after instructor and performer and teaches regularly at some of the worlds largest Belly Dance events like Rakkasah West and East and the Stockholm Belly Dance Festival. She also taught weekly classes at The School of the Art Institute of Chicago 2008-2010. As well, Chellcy has had the pleasure of working with many famous musicians and bands from around the world including Ana Masry Band in Egypt, Karim Nagi in Egypt/USA, Arabesque Orchestra in Toronto, Canada, and many more. Chellcy has also produced her own teaching and performance DVD's and regularly organizes events. Chellcy has devoted her entire life to art, culture and dance. She holds three degrees in art, art history and

Chellcy performing in Budapest, Hungary 2012.

gallery operations from the School of the Art Institute of Chicago and Humboldt State University of CA and has the equivalent of a Minor in Dance. As a writer: in 2000, Chellcy had her own art criticism column in the Arcata Eye newspaper in CA and also won a grant to present her thesis at the San Jose University Art History Symposium. As well she has had several articles published in the Chronicles Belly Dance Magazine. Chellcy is currently pursuing certifications in Flamenco from the Spanish Dance Society of London, Trinity College and now resides on the island of Malta in the E.U. For more information about Chellcy or to contact her please visit her website **www.chellcyraks.com**.

References:

A special thanks to Amaya, Eldridge Saliba-Curmi, George Sawa, Nesma, Karim Nagi, and Puela Lunaris for information, pictures and reference recommendations.

Spanish Dance Society of Trinity College <u>Flamenco Syllabus and Theory</u> Books.
    London. 1994 & 1995 & 1997.

Rossy, Hipolito. Teoria Del Cante Jondo. Editions and Publications, NES,
        1ª,BARCELONA 1966. TAPA DURA EN TELA EDITORIAL, 8°, 1966.

Vittucci, Matteo Marcellus. The Language of Spanish Dance: A Dictionary and
        Reference Manual, Second Edition. Hightstown, NJ: Princeton Book Co.,
        2003.

Sawa, George Dimitri, *Music Performance Practice In The Early 'ABBASID ERA 132-
        320 AH / 750-932 AD,* Second Edition. The Institute of Mediaeval Music,
        Ottawa, Canada ISBN 1-896926-64-9.

La Meri. Spanish Dancing. New York: A.S. Barnes & Company. 1948

Lorca, Federico Garcia. Translated by Maurer, Christopher. Deep Song and Other
        Prose. Marion Boyars, 1980.

The World Book Encyclopedia. World Book-Childcraft International, Inc.
        Merchandise Mart Plaza, Chicago, IL. 1981.

Buonaventura, Wendy, *Serpent of the Nile, Women and Dance in the Arab World.*
        Interlink Books ISBN 1-56656-300-3.

Beach, Milo C., *The Silk Road and Beyond, Travel, Trade, and Transformation.* The Art
    Institute of Chicago / Yale University Press ISBN 978-0-300-12428-6.

Nunez, Juan Carlos Hernandez, Alfredo J. Morales, *The Royal Palace of Seville.* (Real
        Alcazar). Scala Publishers, Spain ISBN 1-85759-201-8.

Ruiz, Ana. Vibrant Andalusia: The Truth About Zambra Mora, 2008.

Amaya's Gypsy Fire documentary

Thomas, Katherine A. *Anda Jaleo, Jaleo! Federico García Lorca and La Argentiníta:
        their song and dance lineage* (paper presentation); 19 February. Los Angeles,
        California: Dance Ethnology Forum. (15th annual)(Paper pending publication.)
        1994.

Encyclopdia Britannica, Encyclopaedia Britannica, 1994, v.8, p.301

Zolan, Simon. *Flamenco Past and Present.*

Pena, Paco. One of his show programs.

Amaya's Gypsy Fire documentary

Websites and Webpages:

Malaguenas Verdiales Malaga Flamenco: a short analysis of flamenco forms in
        Malaga: **http://www.flamencoshop.com/malaga/**

Fandangos de Malaga:
        http://studioflamenco.com/About_Fandangos_de_Malaga.html#abandolaos

Romany People, official website of the International Romani Union acknowledged
        by the United Nations: **http://www.unionromani.org/pueblo_in.htm**

Lorenz, Roberto. *Flamenco – Its Origin and Evolution,* Roberto Lorenz Flamenco
        Page: **http://www.timenet.org/detail.html**

Nesma Al-Andalus Winter Camp. *Nesma and the Andalusi Style*:
        http://www.nesma.us/courses-events/al-andalus-camp/

Olivo, Candela, *Sevillanas, Between Two Worlds*, Flamenco-world.com http://www.flamenco-world.com/magazine/about/sevillana/sevillana.htm

Faucher, Francois. *"The Origins and Development of Flamenco"* in The Guitar
    Foundation of America:
    http://www.classicalguitarmidi.com/history/flamenco.html

Guitar Foundation of America
    <http://www.guitarfoundation.org/>

Flamenco Dance Movement
    http://www.mojacarflamenco.com/About%20Flamenco%20Dance.pdf

Las Flamencas on-line dictionary: **http://flamencotalk.com/Glossary-of-Flamenco**
    terms/Flamenco-Dictionary.html

Hadia, *Spanish Gypsy and Flamenco Dance History*, Centralhome.com, Dance Articles,
    Terms, Definitions, History of Dance, Dance, Fitness and Sports Store:
    http://www.centralhome.com/ballroomcountry/flamenco_history.htm

"The political and artistic impact of Federico Garcia Lorca's *Anda Jaleo* on flamenco
    in Spain and the United States":
    http://www.mojacarflamenco.com/Class%20Handouts/ANDA%20JALEO.pdf

Las Sevillanas, don Quijote Spanish Language Learning
    http://www.donquijote.org/culture/spain/music/sevillanas.asp

House of Names. Swyrich, Archive materials, Swyrich Corporation.
http://www.houseofnames.com/wiki/Moors

Wikimedia Foundation, Inc. Wikipedia, The Free Encyclopedia:
http://en.wikipedia.org/wiki/Flamenco_music
http://en.wikipedia.org/wiki/Flamenco_dance
http://en.wikipedia.org/wiki/Music_of_Aragon
http://en.wikipedia.org/wiki/Andalusia
http://en.wikipedia.org/wiki/Moors
http://en.wikipedia.org/wiki/Maghribi
http://en.wikipedia.org/wiki/Fandango
http://en.wikipedia.org/wiki/Jota_(music)
http://en.wikipedia.org/wiki/Seguidilla
    http://en.wikipedia.org/wiki/Palo_(flamenco)

Aleksu. "Carnival Season: Carnivals kick off in the Basque Country"
    <http://txikilike.blogspot.com/2008_01_01_archive.html>

Evans, Tom and Mary Evans: music, history, construction, and players from the
    Renaissance to Rock

Magnussen, Paul: "Rincon Flamenco No.5: Basic Forms", *Classical Guitar 1997,*: 30-
    33; 47-49.

The Musical Soul of Belly Dance

By Denise Gilbertson

Some philosophers believe that music, or musical tones, are the essence of everything in the universe. Ancient Hindus taught that the "om" is the sound of the universe in harmony with itself. Whatever your beliefs, it is undeniable that music has a profound impact on the human psyche. Like nothing else, music has the power to reach past words and rational thought and touch the emotions, bring up memories or inspire the body to move. As a musician and dancer, for me music has a tremendous significance and impact on my life. Life without music is unimaginable for me and for most humans, I should think!

As dancers we have a particularly rich and inspired relationship to music. In fact, I would say that music IS the soul of our dance. The *raqs sharqi* dancer (or belly dancer if you prefer), strives to make the music visible through the dance. Somehow the accomplished dancer is able to express the rhythm, the melody, the particular tonal qualities of each instrument, the changes and accents in the piece, and the overall emotional content of the music. Music literally "tells" us how to move. And yet there are no hard and fast rules about this. As dance artists in this amazing genre, we are given the freedom to create individual, unique interpretation in our choices of steps, costume, and attitudes. The rule that over-rides every other rule is that the dancer should express a genuine feeling for the music.

Of course, the more one learns about a particular style of music/dance, such as Egyptian or Turkish or American Cabaret, the more one understands the parameters, traditions and concepts of that style. There is always more to learn and always something to learn from native instructors that can't be gained from non-natives. Cultural appropriation is a hot topic of late among dancers. We should always be respectful of the traditions of the dances we perform, and learn as much as we can about them. But if we perform with an honest desire to express the essence of the music, and we make a reasonable effort to learn something about the piece we have chosen (especially the lyrics), I believe that non-native dancers should not hesitate to perform this dance to the music that was created for it, i.e. Egyptian, Turkish or Western Orientale-style music.

In fact, it is my opinion based on 38 years of passionate involvement with the dance, that music, movement and costuming are the three elements that define "belly dance," or *raqs sharqi* if you prefer. In fact, I would go so far as to say that if you are not dancing to music from the cultures of origin, or music created by Western musicians for belly dancers with Middle Eastern rhythms, instruments, maqams, etc., then you may very well not be belly dancing. You may be performing an exciting new style that has exceeded the limits of the "belly dance" definition. The topic of what name to give the many versions of fusion belly dance that have lost nearly all connection with Middle Eastern music, movement and costuming, is hotly debated and is not my focus here. I want to talk about mainstream belly dance and its relationship to the music which is its inspiration and essence. The music and the dance are two aspects of one whole. They are inseparable. And even more than that, when the dancer and the musicians are in synch, connected, there is a synergistic third thing created, an energy that is greater than either the dance or the music by itself. Sometimes this is described as "being in the zone," or "in the groove," or even "going to the temple." Arabs cherish the *tarab,* or the ecstasy of being one with the music. When it occurs, it is a powerful energy that can be felt by everyone in the room. This almost undefinable something often occurs during the *taxim,* (solo musical improvisation) or in the drum solo. In both instances, the dancer and the musician are improvising and playing off the other's energy.

So, as an aspiring Middle Eastern belly dance artist, how can a dancer approach this music which for many of us is not the music we grew up with. My first exposure to Middle Eastern music was a live show with very simple instrumentation – drum and oud – and dancers who played zills. Strangely, though I had never heard music like this before, I felt an instant sense of recognition and attraction to it. The rhythms were clear and compelling and the sound of the oud was beautiful and had an emotional resonance like nothing I had ever heard. The dancers playing finger cymbals were such beautiful, magical creatures to me. I was hooked.

For dancers who want to learn about the music, finding recordings of simple music like that might be a good place to start. When there are only a few instruments playing it is easier to pick out the various components for analysis.

Knowing the basic rhythms of the dance is essential. Learning to play finger cymbals is recommended even if you don't want to dance with them. (In fact, you shouldn't perform with them until you are certain of your skill.) Take a drum or rhythm and zills class to give yourself a good basis to build on. If you have a thorough understanding of the rhythm and can express that in your feet and hips, you have a good foundation for the dance. It is one of the jobs of the belly dancer to illustrate these rhythms with the body, for the audience's enjoyment if they are knowledgeable, and for their edification if they are not familiar with the dance.

Next become familiar with the sound of the oud, with its deep resonant strings; the ney flute, breathy and airy; the kanoon, (also spelled qanun) with its shimmering string sound, and so on. Search YouTube for examples of soloists playing each of these instruments. Dance to the sounds they make and see how they make you feel and move. Internalize the sounds. Create your own signature movement to each instrument – for example, a figure eight of the hips to the oud, a raising of the arms with the ney, a shoulder shimmy to the kanoon. Don't be afraid to play around in the privacy of your own practice. Your devotion to your dance practice will be its own reward – endorphins released! - and will also show in your performances in your comfort level with the music.

The more clearly you can show in your movement the qualities of the sounds you are hearing, the more your audience will understand that your dance is the music made visible. There are so many misconceptions, stereotypes and lack of respect toward our dance. Many people think that belly dance is "just wiggling around in a skimpy costume." If you can demonstrate clearly your connection to the music you will become a good ambassador for our still badly misunderstood art form. And you will be an artist, not just a person in a scandalous outfit who shakes his or her hips!

Attending live music events is highly recommended for anyone who wants to become educated about this dance. If you have an opportunity to perform to live music, step up to the challenge! It

Americanistan L to R: Wayne, Janet Naylor, Denise/Dunyah

can be disconcerting to know that your music won't sound exactly like the recording you have rehearsed to, and that you will have to respond in the moment and make decisions about how to dance. But don't be daunted! Keep in mind that improvisation is an integral part of the musical traditions of Egypt and Turkey. Improvisation was the original root form of the dance as well. By dancing spontaneously you will be right in tune with the many ancestors of the dance of today. If that type of imagery appeals to you, ask your dance idols of the past to help you. You can use choreography if you have opportunities to rehearse with the band or if you know they will play the tune exactly as recorded. And you can use all the knowledge you have gained from dancing choreographies - how to use space, how to vary the movements and so on. But here some ideas to get you comfortable with dancing to live music that can't be choreographed.

Practice dancing spontaneously to random music, to get used to the idea. Attend dance parties and haflas if they are offered in your area. Get up and dance to open dance time at live belly dance music events. Have fun and get relaxed. Get comfortable with Middle Eastern dance music. Listen to it in your car, while you are doing dishes, and as often as possible. You will develop an ear for the rhythms and the changes and the endings and the introductions to the pieces. You will begin to recognize what is the tune and what is the taxim (musical improvisation). Listen to the most famous classic Egyptian dance pieces. There are lists on discussion boards on-line, but here are some common titles: "Aziza," "Zeina," "Alf Leyla wa Leyla," "Leylet Hob," "Habibi Ya Eini," "Tamra Henna." I don't recommend performing improv to these pieces unless you know them extremely well, but by all means practice to them. Let the music sink into your body and your soul.

If you know that you are going to be performing with a particular band, get in touch with them, either through the event organizer or through the band's website. Ask them for a certain piece by name if you can, then practice to their recording of that piece if it is available. Expect that the music will sound different at the live show and that the arrangement of the parts of the piece might even be different. Be prepared to go with the flow. Dance to recordings of the same piece by other artists. Having a rehearsal with the band is great but not always possible.

Do everything you can do build your confidence as a dancer. Keep up with your class attendance, workshops and regular practice. Seek mentorship and coaching from more accomplished dancers. Remind yourself that you don't have to throw every step you know into a performance; in fact it is better if you don't try to do too much. You can repeat a move many times if you are doing it with feeling, conviction and connection to the music. Set an intention for the performance that is meaningful to you. Think of a few movements that you would like to include or a combination that goes particularly well with a certain passage in the piece.

So much of successful performing depends on mental attitude and ability to project emotion and connect with the audience. If you can connect to your music, the musicians and yourself, the audience will feel that. Don't forget to include them as well, of course, through eye contact, facial expressions, gestures, etc. Greatest of all is to perform from a place of love. Love your dance, your music, your musicians, and your audience with all your soul and you will be successful! You will become like the "om," an expression of universal harmony.

About the author: Denise Gilbertson, aka Dunyah, teaches belly dance classes in Eugene, Oregon. She is the director of the band, Americanistan and performs frequently with them. Their music is available online at CDBaby and iTunes. Denise and the band take great pride in the fact that they have introduced many dancers to their first live music performance experience, to almost universally positive response. They also teach workshops on Dancing to Live Music and Rhythms of the Dance for Drummers and Dancers. Contact her at **dunyah@earthlink.net** or see Americanistan's Facebook page. Photo by Natalyn Pepler

American Tribal Style Belly Dance; Third Wave Feminism Shimmies into Popular Culture

By Robin Foster

Imagine the sound of a lone mizmar, a tempo that begins slowly, lazily, as a tribe of four similarly but not identically-dressed women walk in single-file onto the stage, posture erect, chests held high, bare feet lightly gaited but grounded as if to the earth itself. The women come to the center of the stage and, still in queue, form a circle, facing one another, and the melody of the mizmar is joined by the rhythmic beat of eight sets of zils, which click in unison and pick up the tempo. Ba-da-*dum-dum*-duh-duh-duh-duh-duh-duh-*dum*, ba-da-*dum-dum*-duh-duh-duh-duh-duh-*dum*. The woman are dressed in rich jewel-toned fabrics – floor-length full velvet skirts, each made from at least ten yards of fabric; under the skirts, which one can see when the dancers spin, are silk pantaloons, saffron yellows and garnet reds; triangular hip scarves made from mirrored fabric dangle fringed tassels which sway left and right with the pop of the hips; choli tops, with backs bare, cover the arms and chest and are accented with coin bras and heavy Afghani-inspired jewelry; finally, scarves wrapped around the head in turbans – an item never worn by women in the Middle East – require the dancers to hold a firm posture and are also adorned with jewels and pins. The dancers each have extensive tattoos down the arms, across the backs and torsos. The dancers' eye makeup would make Elizabeth Taylor proud.

As the women form a circle, the dance begins in earnest. As if on cue - the audience may not know that American Tribal Style belly dance is almost always an improvised dance, not choreographed – the four dancers align in a diamond shape, face the audience, and begin a series of identical hip circles, arm postures, turns, hip drops, and torso undulations. Two dancers move up and two dancers move back. The dancers turn to the right in a full circle, drop the hips in an alternating shimmy, and then rise up on the balls of the feet and turn back around again. All of these dance moves occur in unison to an up-tempo beat of the doumbek and the ba-da-*dum-dum*-duh-duh-duh-duh-duh-duh-*dum* of the dances' zils. Frequently the dancers re-form their circle and dance as they move in a clockwise rotation, eyes on one another, until at some point – again, this is all purely improvised and the dancers must watch each other for subtle hand signals which will cue a change in the dance – the troupe faces the audience yet again. This is American Tribal Style belly dance, performed by Carolena Nerrichio and her troupe, Fatchancebellydance, in San Francisco, 2009. This is not the *hootchy-kootchy* dance of early twentieth century burlesque and vaudeville shows and if there were no audience members present, these women would perform this dance in the same manner, for themselves and for each other. American Tribal Style belly dance is, among other things, a product of feminism, a celebration of female strength and camaraderie.

Belly dance, the term coined at the 1893 Chicago World's Fair, has a complicated history in American popular culture. Long before it was brought to the West during the world's fair expositions of the late nineteenth and early twentieth centuries, the dance of the "harem girls" was represented in Western art and literature as a provocative tradition from the "exotic" Middle East, performed by alluring objects (women) meant to titillate male subjects. However, representations of belly dance in the West as a sexualized performance meant to satisfy the male gaze does not adequately explain the meanings imbued in the dance for contemporary women who participate in and perform American Tribal Style dance. The rise of ATS in popular culture follows First, Second, and Third Wave feminism across the twentieth century, rooted in conceptions of female empowerment and a focus on sisterhood. ATS specifically rejects Orientalist sexualized representations of "dancing girls" performing for male pleasure; instead, the dancers' focus is on the other members of the tribe and is rooted in an ideology of collective female strength.

The transformation and evolution of belly dance in America coincides with feminist movements that have each sought to free American women from traditional gender norms and conceptions of appropriate feminine identity. This essay examines Orientalist representations of belly dance and "harem girls" in the West during the age of European colonization in the Middle East and through the dance's earliest performances in American culture at the turn of the twentieth century. Rejecting sexualized representations of the dance across the previous century, American Tribal Style evolved as a reappropriation of earlier forms of belly dance; a feminist project that seeks to reclaim the performance of the dance from its Orientalist-inspired introduction in the West.

REPRESENTATIONS OF BELLY DANCE IN WESTERN ART AND PERFORMANCE

It was a curious and wonderful gymnastic. There was no graceful dancing- only the movement of dancing when she advanced, throwing one leg before the other as gypsies dance. But the rest was most voluptuous motion – not the lithe wooing of languid passion, but the soul of passion starting through every sense, and quivering in every limb.
– G.W Curtis, London. 1852

Neither the origins of belly dance nor the origins of the perception of professional dancers as participants in a dishonorable profession are clearly defined in the historic record. The English word "dance" comes from the Sanskrit *tanha*, meaning "joy of life," while *raks*, Arabic, and *rakkase,* Turkish, are both derivations from the Assyrian *rakadu,* which means, "to celebrate." While not all sources agree, general consensus among belly dancers and musicians locates the origin of the dance in pre-Islamic religious worship and celebration, during a period when religious and/or spiritual practice was more fully integrated into daily life. Shay and Sellers-Young caution against ascribing religious origins to Middle Eastern dance, or any form of dance for that matter. "No one can write with certainty about dance practices that occurred thousands of years ago; dance may not have been a feature of religious life throughout the entire Middle East, much less the Orient." Whether originating from religious sources, as a birthing ritual, or simply as a form of secular entertainment, from the regions of Greece, Cadiz, Persia, and ancient Egypt references to a *dance of the hips* have been recorded since Napoleon's conquest of Egypt (1798-1801) and the age of Orientalism. As Islam began to dominate much of the Middle East, Persia, and India during the seventh century A.D., the ethical principals of the religion condemned female dance in public and all dance became relegated to the secular sphere. Female dancers, often gypsies, who did not conform to the cultural norms of Islam were regarded with suspicion and derision by the faithful. The entertainer/dancer became an unacceptable occupation for respectable women.

Nineteenth century European travelers to the Middle East left numerous records of their encounters with the "exotic" dancers. Dancers were represented as a sexualized symbol of the Oriental *other*; exotic, titillating, performing for male pleasure. James Augustus St. John, English painter, travelled to Cairo in 1845 and wrote of a performance by "dancing girls" in the private home of a wealthy Armenian:

> Their eyes shot fire; their bosoms heaved and panted, and their bodies assumed the most varied attitudes and inflexions. They twined round each other snake-like, with a suppleness and grace such as I have never seen before. Now, they let their arms drop, and their whole frames seemed to collapse in utter exhaustion; then might you see how a new thought arose within them, and strove to express itself in impassioned gestures. All this while the music continued to play, and in its very simplicity was like a pale background to the picture, from which the glowing figures of the girls stood out in so much the stronger relief.

St. John's descriptions of the Cairo dancing girls were by no means uncorroborated. French writer Gustave Flaubert travelled through Upper Egypt in 1849-51. In private letters to Louis Bouilhet, Flaubert recounts the dance of the *ghawazi* in the throes of the fevered Dance of the Bee. In this dance, the gypsy dancer creates the pantomime of frantically searching for a bee trapped inside her clothing as she removes her garments one by one. This spectacle of woman-as-object performing for a male patron is similar to that of the male gaze encountered in visual art. The female representing a passive sexualized object, performing for the amusement and pleasure of the masculine gaze is typical of the European traveler's account of the performance of Middle Eastern dance and reproduces the larger colonial dynamic of the period.

Image 1: *Dance of the Bee in the Harem, by Vincenzo Marinelli. 1862. Oil on canvas. Museo e gallerie nazionali di Capodimonte. Photo courtesy of ARTStor digital database.*

A century of titillating description, both in written form and in visual art, had become the mode of representation of Middle Eastern dance in Western popular culture prior to the arrival of actual Middle Eastern female dancers in the United States. These representations of the exotic, eroticized female came to represent, for many Americans, Arab culture *in situ.* That no Western man would have ever set foot inside a harem, as is implied in Marinelli's painting above, is irrelevant. This representation of the bare-breasted, sultry woman, in the throes of hyper-sexualized fervor and sexually available for the pleasure of the privileged voyeur, precedes the arrival of actual belly dancers in America by several decades. During the middle-to-late nineteenth century, Middle Eastern dancers were exhibited as spectacles at many of the world's trade and commerce fairs. London's Crystal Palace Exhibition in 1851, New York's Crystal Palace Exhibition in 1853, and Chicago's Great Columbian Exposition of 1893 each included staged re-creations of markets and villages from across the globe. In addition to a Moorish palace and Turkish and Persian theaters, the Chicago's World's Fair presented Middle Eastern dancers from Egypt, Syria, and Algeria.

Throngs packed the fair's beer gardens, thrilled to see the Ferris Wheel, and gaped as the belly dancer Fahreda Mahzar – also known as "Little Egypt" – gyrated in ways never before witnessed by middle-class Americans. And Little Egypt was by no means the only belly dancer on that earlier Midway. Other "Orientals" performed sexual spectacles wearing native costumes that revealed considerable more skin than visitors ever saw in a mainstream woman's magazine (Ganz, 2008).

These Arabic-inspired village re-creations and live dancers were presented to American audiences in marked contrast to delicate Victorian sensibilities. Westerners flocked to see the performance of a dance that had been depicted in the writings and visual art of European travelers during the previous century. Witnesses to the dance found the performances shocking, indecent and offensive; the performance of "Little Egypt," who "gyrated in ways never before witnessed by middle-class Americans," was pure spectacle. An attempt by Bertha Palmer, President of the Board of Lady Managers, to have the Chicago venue closed down for indecency increased the public furor over the controversy and only attracted more attention, bolstering flagging ticket sales. The dancers' venue became the most popular site on the Midway. This "belly dance," a term coined by Midway promoter Sol Bloom during the Chicago World's Fair to describe the entirety of dances from Persia, Egypt, Morocco and Tunisia, became equated in American popular culture with seductive titillation. Following the 1893 exhibition, the *danse du ventre* appeared in carnival sideshows, burlesque houses, and on the vaudeville stage.

While the dance was completely sexualized and indeed a precursor to the later striptease, Hollywood began to cash in on the hootchy-cootchy craze by showcasing the Oriental dance on stage and screen. When Hollywood starlets such as Maude Allen, Ruth St. Denis and Isadora Duncan brought the exotic, Middle Eastern dance to such American productions as *Salome* (1908) and *Egypta* (1913), and Josephine Baker performed Middle East-inspired dance in the French productions *ZouZou* (1934) and *Princess Tam Tam* (1935), performance of the dance was already undergoing transformation and hybridization. These American actresses, trained in the classical dances and steeped in a sense of modernism with an altogether different set of gender norms, consciously or unconsciously altered the body language of the dances performed by Little Egypt and her imitators into what would be referred to as Egyptian cabaret-style belly dance.

"These productions helped to create the widespread idea of exotic dance as representation of the Middle Eastern woman," and it was the Western woman, in fact, who became the "face" of belly dance in the United States.

A cultural exploration of belly dance cannot continue without some acknowledgment of the ways in which the popularization of the dance in the West grew in relation to early Orientalist conceptions. While my argument that belly dance's rise in popularity among middle-class American women has occurred as a manifestation of feminist ideology does not discount an exotic lure which was clearly a part of the West's early fascination with the dance, a strictly Orientalist paradigm, which scholars have relied upon to examine the appropriation of belly dance in the West, does not sufficiently address this correlation. Several scholars have analyzed the representation of the Middle Eastern woman via Western performance of belly dance through an Orientalist framework, situating the performance of Western belly dance as a problematic cultural form, complicit in perpetuating stereotypes and solidifying perceptions of *Otherness*.

While the initial presentation of the *danse du ventre* in the West was certainly mired in cultural stereotyping and titillating spectacle, the hybridization and performance of the dance by middle-class women was fueled by burgeoning waves of feminist ideology during the course of the twentieth century. Further, the ideology of Orientalism is itself problematic, and not accepted as sufficient by a number of scholars well versed in the study of the culture and politics of the Middle East and East-West relations. Certainly the two paradigms of Orientalism and feminism can exist simultaneously, and one does not necessarily negate the other. While this author acknowledges the themes of Orientalism which gave rise to the production and performance of belly dance in American at the turn of the twentieth century, the projects of Second and Third Wave feminism provide greater insight into the dance form's rise in respectability amongst middle-class women and in American popular culture.

During the first half of the twentieth century, a particular style of costume and body language became typical of belly dance performers and performances across the country. Robert Henri's *Salome* (1909) captures a chiffon-draped, barely-covered dancer, whose posture is more reminiscent of a ballerina than of the dancers gawked at on the Midway in 1893:

For many Western women who were performing this new dance form in America, the attraction of belly dance was in direct opposition to the passivity represented in Henri's painting. Posed in a cabaret-style costume of sheer chiffon, legs scandalously visible beneath the flimsy material, with foot on pointe a la the ballerina, Henri's *Salome* presented an image of the belly dancer to the Western viewer and remained her iconic representation throughout much of the century. The exposed body, swinging fringe, and reflecting sequins became representative of the female body as much as the movement itself. In fact, by the 1965 debut of the television show *I Dream of Jeannie,* this image had remained much the same in American popular culture and this was the dominant representation of the belly dancer in America through much of the twentieth century. However, while Henri's *Salome* appears docile and placid, with her eyes lowered in gaze so as not to assume any sort of agency herself, many Western dancers were attracted to the dance precisely because through this dance, they were able to express a femininity not accepted in the traditional gender norms of the day.

Image 2: *Salome, by Robert Henri. 1909. Oil on canvas. The Ringling Museum of Art, the State Art Museum of Florida. Photo courtesy of ARTStor, digital database*

During the Progressive Era, Western romantic associations of the Orient with a pre-modern simplicity, purity and naturalness were admired in middle-class aesthetics for their purported anti-modern sensibilities. Due in large part to the transformative effects of the Industrial Revolution, the consumption of Eastern art and performance was viewed as a culturally refining influence on white, middle-class society. Through the consumption of exotic forms of art and dance, middle class American women were afforded an opportunity to travel vicariously, thereby expanding their limited domestic sphere. In effect, consumption of Eastern material culture and performance signaled the New Woman of the Progressive Era, challenging the strict gender norms of the Victorian Age.

It was not incidental that these Orientalist performances by white women took place at the same time that many white women were becoming New Women of the twentieth century, who challenged Victorian gender norms and the ideology of the separate spheres by participating in the women's suffrage movement, demanding birth control, engaging in socialism, expressing themselves in art and letters, seeking "free love," cutting their hair and smoking cigarettes. The construction of such a new gender identity was closely linked to, and was articulated through, enacting roles and identities other than their own. The performance of Asian femininity thus provided an effective tool for white women's empowerment and pleasure as a New Woman.

Wrapped up in the feminist project of the early twentieth century, what would become known as First Wave feminism, was the demand by predominantly white middle-class women to expand their relegation from the private sphere into public life in new, non-normative ways. Yoshihara argues that white American women's fascination with cultural products depicting an alternative style of femininity allowed these American women to construct new identities for themselves, providing liberation from the strict gender norms of the Victorian era. Maude Allen's performance of *Salome* in an onstage performance of Oscar Wilde's 1891 tragic play, signaled a subtle transformation from the manner in which the voyeuristic gaze had come to typify representations of Middle Eastern women through dance and performance. In this onstage production, Allen's *Salome* invites the voyeuristic gaze from the audience while at the same time asserts her triumph and pleasure over the severed head of John the Baptist. The *Salome* craze swept across American and Europe in the first decade of the twentieth century, imitated and replicated in cities from Paris to San Francisco. In each case, the female dancer represented not merely a fetish for the male gaze, but also portrayed herself as a "vehicle for self-expression and sexual assertiveness onstage, often morphing the role in dynamic ways." In this way, the portrayal of Salome became a vehicle "to claim possession of their own erotic gaze, albeit a hostile and aggressive one."

4946 M ROTARY PHOTO, E.C.   MISS MAUD ALLAN,   FOULSHAM & BANFIELD
                                                AS " SALOME."

Image 3: *Maude Allen as Salome, 1896*

While mainstream American audiences would continue to equate belly dancing with sexual wantonness and salaciousness throughout much of the twentieth century, it is critical to this analysis that we make the distinction between popular perceptions in American culture on the one hand, and the ideology of feminism, agency and the expansion of gender norms heralded by predominantly white female dancers on the other. When Simone de Beauvoir posed her infamous question in 1952, *What is a woman?* she was addressing the unfinished business of the First Wave of feminism. While these early Progressive Era advocates intended to expand acceptable conceptions of womanhood and femininity by participating in the women's suffrage movement, demanding access to birth control, engaging in socialism, and bobbing their hair and smoking cigarettes, circumstances for most women remained, on the whole, confining. The manner in which "woman" had been and would be defined remained a critical project of feminist discourse. Performing and admiring this new and still unusual "exotic" dance became a vehicle by which some American woman exacted agency and demanded a more complicated and expansive sphere of acceptable gender norms.

BELLY DANCE AND CULTURAL FEMINISM OF THE 1970s

While popular conceptions of belly dance remained steeped in images of sexual wantonness carried over from the early Orientalist portrayals of Egyptian and Turkish dancing girls from the nineteenth century, many American woman who were attracted to the dance found exhilaration in the expanded physical freedom not found in traditional European dance genres. To many early feminists, the new form of bodily expression made available through belly dance was a liberating experience signaling the arrival of the New Woman of the Progressive Era. However, continued public perception of the dance as salacious, and the increasing appearance of belly dance in risqué burlesque shows, denigrated the public reputation of the dance to no better than a strip-tease. By the 1960s the performance of belly dance in America was predominantly of the cabaret-style: sheer costumes, hootchy-kootchy mannerisms, overtly sexualized, performed in seedy establishments on the fringes of city limits. Why the performance of this dance remained predominantly a scandalous form of entertainment is a complex question but one that is not unique to belly dance. Historically, entertainers have long assumed a base reputation in societies across the globe, and regardless of the feminist spirit of some of America's first Middle-Eastern inspired dancers, public perceptions held fast to a salacious characterization of the dance.

The 1960 -70s witnessed a shift in perceptions of belly dance, attracted more women to the dance form, and experienced a resurgence in popularity with the rise of the Second Wave feminist movement of those decades. Belly dance remained, on the whole, a sexualized and fetishized performance at the dawn of the rebellious '60s. As feminists of the Second Wave sought to reappropriate the dance and claim ownership for themselves, "a number of dancers in the 1970s turned towards rhetorical and performative strategies that resisted the seductive image of the dancer by emphasizing the experience of female community and the ethnic roots of the dance. The tribal dynamic has its foots in the rejection of the particular set of seductive relationships between audience and dancer." While in the early twentieth century many white middle-class American women were drawn to the material culture, art, and performances of the East as a means to vicariously experience cultural aspects of the Orient, actual travel to the East witnessed a boom in the 1960s. As Kraus explains, "The American public's interest in diverse spiritual paths continued to grow, and it has been argued that images of the 'mystic East' assisted Americans with spiritual needs Western religions were not meeting." Innovations in transportation, specifically air travel, made world travel a physical possibility for more

Americans than steam liners had previously allowed. In addition, social movements of the 1960s rejected a constricted Victorian-inspired conception of the human body and, combined with the availability of air travel, promoted expanding norms of gender identity, spiritual exploration, and appropriate body language. Sellers-Young characterizes Second Wave feminism by its focus on the "body as a site of pleasure and discovery," especially among white liberal feminists.

Several scholars, including Barbara Sellers-Young, Sunaima Maira and Stavros Stavrou Karayanni, have examined this connection between ethnicity and the popularization of belly dance in the West. Maira argues that race and ethnicity are integral factors in any examination of the performance of belly dance and concludes that while "women of color may have a different relationship to belly dancing and connect to it via a notion of cultural similarity, rather than cultural difference," it appears that women of color nonetheless are attracted to belly dance as a social and spiritual outlet in much the same manner as are middle-class white women, "as a social avenue to meet other women and a way to fashion their own femininity in the context of the middle-class American sisterhood it offers." The attraction to the dance, therefore, appears more closely aligned with class lines than those of ethnicity or race.

The project of cultural feminism is integral to understanding this transformation of belly dance during the 1960s and 70s. Cultural feminism, "the ideology of a female nature or female essence reappropriated by feminists themselves in an effort to revalidate undervalued female attributes," focuses on an essentialist nature of woman and became a counter-ideology to the radical feminism of the 1970s. Professor of Philosophy Linda Alcoff cites Mary Daly and Adrienne Rich as influential proponents of cultural feminism in the academic literature, in which part of the project was to break from "the trend toward androgyny and the minimizing of gender differences that was popular among feminists in the early 1970s." Both Daly and Rich argue for the essential female character of women, in which Daly claims the natural essence (whether biological or socialized in origin) of the female spirit requires recharging through bonding with other women, must be "freed from male parasites," and seeks a free space where creativity and expression can thrive. Likewise, Rich argues for the essential femaleness of woman, which originates in her power to give life, and is the focus of male "envy, awe, and dread." Both Daly and Rich advise that women must break free of the subjugation of patriarchy and can achieve this only through collective bonding with other women and the essential female spirit. Whether or not the reader agrees with the ideology of cultural feminism as espoused by Rich and Daly, the implications for the feminist movement in the 1970s must be considered. In its valorization of female attributes, focus on universal and essential conceptions of womanhood, and in the call to repossession by women of their bodies, cultural feminism sought to bring deep change to civilization, develop new meanings within the relationships between men and women, and affect the balance of power in both the personal and public spheres.

Critics of cultural feminism cite many limitations, including claims that this movement is ahistorical, homogeneous, and the product of white feminists. Indeed, its focus on essentialism receives some of the strongest attacks: "To the extent that [cultural feminism] reinforces essentialist explanations of these attributes, it is in danger of solidifying an important bulwark for sexist oppression." Determining the usefulness of the project of cultural feminism is an examination outside the scope of this study; instead of critiquing its role in advancing the equality of women, we must examine the resurgence of belly dance within the historical and cultural framework of the 1970s and the growing popularity of cultural feminism at that time. Belly dancers who cite feelings of empowerment, sisterhood, and becoming a part of the collective power of women, were each ascribing to some notion of cultural feminism and this helps to explain the new direction that belly dance began to take in the 1970s.

In its popular practice, belly dance is broadly construed as a form of personal expression rooted in a kind of liberal humanist feminism and governed by notions of women's experience as universal. Practitioners often describe belly dancing as a natural expression of gender that is unique to women, with gender understood to be a stable, heteronormative category.

AMERICAN TRIBAL STYLE IN THE NEW FEMINISM

Western belly dance is clearly not "just dance." For many practitioners, belly dance gives women's bodies an expressive identity not available elsewhere. The aesthetics of the dance become a form of resistance against the alienation from the body perceived to be a function of Western modernization. Out of Orientals' frustrations with backward societies, belly dancing recoups notions of ancient spiritualities, woman-centered environments, access to hidden knowledge, and the universality of women's experience.

Jamila Salimpour learned Egyptian style dance by watching *Ghawazee* dancers perform in Egypt and by watching Egyptian movies as a child living in Egypt. In the 1960s she danced and taught at the Baghdad Cabaret in San Francisco, an establishment she owned. Salimpour hired Middle Eastern dancers from various countries to perform for her predominantly male clientele, and she watched and learned how to fuse a variety of dance forms into a single performance. Her troupe, Bal-Anat, began to infuse styles of dance outside the typical repertoire of Egyptian cabaret, including influences from Algerian, Turkish, and Spanish flamenco style dances. This new dance form, not yet named, began to be imitated across the United States. Jamila says of her early fusion style, "Indeed, many people thought it was the real thing, when in fact it was half real and half hokum."

This allusion to the "real thing" speaks to charges of cultural appropriation by Westerners of an Eastern dance form. In a transnational circulation of culture, how is authenticity determined? Where lies the essential nature of any cultural form? As charges of essentialism have been exacted against the ideology of cultural feminism, so too must an essentialist framework be critically examined in any charges of cultural appropriation. Salimpour's fusion of a variety of European and Middle Eastern dance styles created a transformation in the dance, one that combined a variety of styles and techniques from the culturally and ethnically diverse dancers who came to perform at the Baghdad Cabaret. The cultural climate of San Francisco in the 1960s is an important component in our analysis of the evolution of belly dance from a sexy burlesque romp into a tribe of sisterhood celebrating female empowerment. While the counterculture movement gained momentum during the 1960s in cities across America, none experienced the rebellious demands of counterculture as completely as did San Francisco's Bay Area.

The beats, hippies, and gays represented a very un-genteel sort of bohemianism that was more confrontational, more political, and more bizarre than ever before in this country. The New

Bohemianism was absolutely critical in forming the political consciousness and urbane outlook of the Bay Area, moving the middle class decisively to the left of American mainstream.

The Bay Area's hippie/bohemian/counterculture movement, while itself remaining outside of mainstream American middle class culture, expanded the boundaries of middle class sexual, political and cultural norms in that region. This had significant implications on the rise of belly dance's popularity amongst the middle class in the 1960s and 1970s Bay Area.

Masha Archer studied dance under Salimpour and her troupe, Bal-Anat. In the early 1970s Archer founded her own troupe, the San Francisco Classic Dance Troupe. Under Archer's direction, this new fusion-style belly dance became even more eclectic than at Bal-Anat. "We looked like some sort of European, Parisian-Tunisians with a very strong Byzantine tribal look, which was completely invented." Archer called her style "Authentic Modern American," a term which nodded to the American tendency to appropriate and transform foreign cultural forms in order to create a new American experience. Archer was not only a dancer, but a strong proponent of feminist ideology and spirit. The most important facet of her teaching method was not the dance technique itself, but teaching her students "there is nothing more beautiful and more dignified than you are."

Carolena Nericcio began studying with Archer at the age of fourteen and started her own dance troupe, Fatchancebellydance, in San Francisco in 1987. It was during FCBD's earliest years as a dance troupe when the term American Tribal Style was coined. When asked where the term originated, Nericcio responds, "It may have been to clarify that we're not trying to imitate a specific tribe, we're definitely American people who enjoy this dance form and we're not claiming to be authentic." Specifically, ATS seeks to reject the early performance of belly dance as a provocative, overtly sexualized representation of a passive female performing for the salacious pleasure of a voyeuristic (male) audience. While the roots of ATS are grounded in the gypsy dances of the Middle East, the fusion with Spanish flamenco, Indian mudras, Goth and punk fashions of the American club scene combines to create the unique presentation of this dance. Critical to ATS is the collective focus on the tribe of dancers; "A tribal setting facilitates a collective re-examination of ideals of beauty; as well as the individual space for each woman to define and pursue her own ideal of beauty and fitness."

Not only is American Tribal Style a remarkably different dance, both in tempo and in form, from the Egyptian-style cabaret that most Americans are familiar with due to representations of belly dance in media and popular culture, the look of the dancers is dramatically altered and reflects a shift away from a sexualized focus on the sultry female form. The skirt is floor-length, made of ten yards of fabric, and the legs are covered with silk pantaloons. The dancers are usually barefoot, eschewing the high heels that quickly became part of the Hollywood look of the cabaret dancer of the 1920s. While the midriff is bare, the arms are covered and décolletage is not part of the costume. Jewelry, decorative pins, and tattoos create an impossible-to-classify amalgamation of personal adornment.

Further, a woman does not need to have the figure of a ballerina nor of a busty burlesque performer; modern belly dance accepts a far broader range of body types than can be found in traditional forms of Western dance, including ballet and modern dance. A 2010 study by

Downey, Reel, SooHoo and Zerbib found that "the overwhelming majority of dancers surveyed [92.1%], indicated that participation in the dance had a positive influence on how they feel about their body." Not only did survey respondents indicate that participation in a belly dance class promotes a collective appreciation for the well-being of women in general, the performance of the dance by a variety of body types challenges normative ideas about the ideal female form. Like the Progressive Era New Women before them, these dancers are committed to challenging normative gender roles and cultural ideas about femininity and dominant body image norms.

The late twentieth century rise in popularity of American Tribal Style belly dance troupes across the country – indeed, ATS troupes can be found from Scottsdale Arizona to St. Louis Missouri and New York City – coincides with the transition from the Second Wave feminist movement to the Third Wave in the late 1980s. Power feminists of the Third Wave reject some of the limiting aspects they saw in Second Wave feminism, including what many regard as a "prudish feminism" and radical politics that were often critical of explicitly gendered roles, subjects, and sexuality. Globalization and an increasing influence of mass culture have impacted this shift wherein "many younger [Third Wave] feminists celebrate contradictions as a means of resistance to identity of categorization, much in the spirit of performance theories and queer theorists."

While the new fusion style of belly dance practiced by Salimpour and Archer in San Francisco in the 1960s and 70s experienced a surge in local popularity, the more widespread appeal of ATS exploded across the country in the 1990s with the growth of this "new" feminism. In very cursory description, Third Wave feminism departs from and challenges its predecessor, which many new feminist critics find dominating, exclusive and restricting. New feminists of the Third Wave appreciate a more open and fluid gendered sexuality, where labels appear less definitive, and the modern feminist has freedom to play with ideas of gender and sexuality in ways that many radical feminists of the 1970s rejected. Whereas radical feminists of the Second Wave exclaimed, "You can't tear down the master's house with the master's tools," new feminists of the Third Wave are perfectly comfortable using their specifically female physical attributes if it serves personal, while not necessarily political, goals. Author Marcelle Karp encourages women to use "our tits and hips and lips" as "power tools" in the new world order. In a similar vein, Elizabeth Wurtzel states, "These days putting our one's pretty power, one's pussy power, one's sexual energy for popular consumption no longer makes you a bimbo. It makes you smart." The sexual assertiveness of pop starlets Shakira and Britney Spears, who have each incorporated belly dance into their music videos, has further integrated the dance into popular youth culture. Third Wave feminism appears to especially revel in the rebelliousness of subverting traditional gender norms and categories, even those previously broadened by earlier feminists.

If the rise of Third Wave feminism can help explain the environment in which American Tribal Style belly dance has exploded in popularity in the last two decades, and can create a context in which many American women now situate themselves in the new world order, then we can see how ATS is in fact less about belly dance and more specifically about female celebration and empowerment. Nericcio feels that Fatchancebellydance and ATS are, for the most part "about female positivity. It's a celebration of all the positive aspects of the feminine and it wants to celebrate the female body in a really upright and uplifted and bright form." ATS has emerged as a social, communal and feminist form of dance that runs counter to the historical narrative of a solo exotic dance performed for the pleasure of a male audience (in fact, most audience members at ATS performances are couples, family groups, and women). The tribal aspect of ATS is a critical component in distinguishing itself from its cabaret-style predecessors, in which a solo dancer performs for her audience. In ATS, the dancer's performance: is witnessed and validated by the chorus of women dancing behind her – they form a counter-audience to the one on the other side of the stage, their appreciative presence both guiding the spectator in how to respond and implicitly pointing out that his opinion is not the only, nor the most important, one. Fat Chance thus presents an image of feminine sociality, rather than seduction, onstage. The gaze is de-fetishized, becoming a medium of communication and exchange between dancers in a circuit that includes the audience but does not pander to it.

It is this focus on the collective tribe of dancers that creates an atmosphere of sisterly camaraderie, a major appeal to many women who participate in ATS dance troupes across the country. Reminiscent of the politics of cultural feminism of the 1970s, many ATS dancers cite this connection with a universal female energy as being a critical attraction of the dance:

For me, tribal dancing reveals the awesome power and beauty of the female archetype. The bounty of love and goodwill that glows from this shared appreciation for one another leads me to a spiritual reverence for the pure sensuous dignity of women dancing together – Kim White, San Francisco

I love being connected to a community of women in this way and appreciating the beauty, spirit, and strength of every woman – Sahar, Missouri

I think of these other women around the world, who think about the same things I do: children, family, making ends meet, the joy of a baby, being a mommy, being in love. And dancing! I hear the shimmy of a coin belt and I smile. It connects me with so many other women. I guess you could say I understand the world better and feel more a part of a stream of creative human expression and womanhood across time and distance – Anya, Missouri

It's a very sisterly thing to belly dance; it celebrates life and femaleness. It is also a non-competitive form of dance. It develops a woman's trust and confidence in expressing her body openly and freely. – Coco Daly, Sydney Australia

Belly dancing allows a woman to express her deepest innermost soul. It's a way of releasing each woman's own unique energy, allowing her to interpret of herself who she is at that moment. – Yaeli-Yael Gilboa-Nomis, Jerusalem

CONCLUDING REMARKS

American Tribal Style belly dance has succeeded in breaking into mainstream American popular culture as a respectable dance form over the course of the last two decades. The dance's focus on the tribe, and its refusal to pander to a voyeuristic male gaze creates a feeling of solidarity among the dancers and is rooted in feelings of female empowerment and strength. Viewed within a framework of cultural and Third Wave feminism, ATS has entered into the public sphere through the women who have continued to challenge norms of appropriate female identity. The founder of Fatchancebellydance, Carolena Nericcio, insists that the feminist spirit of the dance comes from dedication to the physical and spiritual strength of the women who perform the dance and retains the focus of the dance in the collective strength of these women. Likewise, many female participants are drawn to the dance because, within this shared space, attitudes concerning what is acceptable, appropriate, or beautiful continually push the boundaries of traditional gender norms. In their 2010 study on body image in belly dance, Downey, Reel, SooHoo and Zerbib's concluded:

All of [these findings] suggest preconditions for at least some measure of alternative (if not oppositional) consciousness among belly dancers such that challenges to dominant body type image norms are contextualized within broader challenges to gender structures. Moreover, it offers an important piece of data to the debates over whether belly dance is supportive of or oppositional to feminist projects; it certainly suggests that among belly dancers there is greater support for feminism than among the population generally. These data suggest that belly dance provides a space to promote alternative norms more attuned to the needs and realities of women precisely because men are (largely) absent.

By re-appropriating and re-characterizing the salacious dance of the early twentieth century, twenty-first century feminists reclaim the performance of belly dance for personal – including physical, spiritual, and communal - satisfaction. In this way, the personal is political; personal empowerment derived from the collaborative performance of American Tribal Style belly dance serves to expand accepted gender norms and engages with the political ideology of Third Wave feminism in declaring *sisters are doin' it for themselves.*

BIBLIOGRAPHY

Alcoff, Linda. "Cultural Feminism versus Post-Structuralism: The Identity Crisis in Feminist Theory," Signs, Vol. 13, No. 3 (Spring, 1988) 405-436.

Alexis, India & Meaghan Madges. "A Dance of Her Own; FCBD proves that the female figure, no matter what size, can be sexy," *Dance Magazine*, Nov. 2002. p. 52

Bentley, Toni. *Sisters of Salome* (New Haven: Yale University Press. 2002)

Briggs, David. "Belly dancing as a vehicle for spiritual exploration," *National Catholic Reporter.* January 11, 2008.

Brook, James, Chris Carlsson & Nancy Peters. *Reclaiming San Francisco; History, Politics, Culture* (San Francisco: City Lights Books. 1998)

Bouchard, Pierre Louis. *Les Almées* (1893). Oil on canvas. Musée d'Orsay, Paris. Photo courtesy ARTStor digital database.

Buonaventura, Wendy. *Serpent of the Nile; Women and Dance in the Arab World* (New York: Interlink Books, 1998)

Desai, Manisha. "The Messy Relationship Between Feminisms and Globalizations," Gender and Society, Vol. XX, No. X (2007). 1-7.

Djoumahna, Kajira. "Ignorance is Bliss; an interview with Carolena Nericcio, Instructor & Director of FatChanceBellyDance of San Francisco," *Crescent Moon Magazine* (March-April 1996)

Downey, Reel, SooHoo and Zerbib , "Body Image in Belly dance: integrating alternative norms into collective identity," *Journal of Gender Studies,* Vol. 19 No. 4 (Dec. 2010)

Dox, Donnalee. "Dancing Around Orientalism," *The Drama Review* 50:4 (T192) Winter 2006. 52-71.

FatChanceBellyDance videos

Downey, Dennis J., Justine J. Reel, Sonya SooHoo and Sandirine Zerbib. "Body Image in Belly dance: integrating alternative norms into collective identity," *Journal of Gender Studies,* Vol. 19 No. 4 (Dec. 2010)

Ganz, Cheryl. *The 1933 Chicago's World Fair; A Century of Progress* (Chicago: The University of Illinois Press, 2008).

Gohil, Neha Singh. "American belly dancers are rescuing a Middle Eastern tradition," *Columbia News Service,* February 27, 2007.

Gordon, Jane. "Moving with the spirit of Salome," *New York Times,* May 21, 2006.

Guthrie, Julian. "Belly dancers strut stuff in Richmond," *The San Francisco Chronicle,* March 16, 1997.

Halliday, Fred. "'Orientalism' and Its Critics," *British Society for Middle Eastern Studies,* Vol. 20 No. 2 (1993) 145-163.

Henri, Robert. *Salome* (1909). Oil on canvas. The Ringling Museum of Art, the State Art Museum of Florida. Photo courtesy of ARTStor, digital database.

Keft-Kennedy, Virginia. "How Does She Do That? Belly Dancing and the Horror of a Flexible Woman," *Women's Studies,* 34: 279-300

Kenny, Erin. "Belly dance in the Town Square; Leaking Peace through Tribal Style Identity," *Western Folklore* 66: 3 & 4 (Summer & Fall 2007) 301-327.

Kinser, Amber E. "Negotiating Spaces For/Through Third-Wave Feminism," *NWSA Journal,* Vol. 16, No. 3 (Fall, 2004) 124-153.

Kraus, Rachel. "Straddling the Sacred and the Secular: Creating a Spiritual Experience Through Belly Dance," Sociological Spectrum, Vol. 29, No. 5 (2009) 598-625.

Nericcio, Carolena. *Tribal Talk; A Retrospective, The Voice of FatChanceBellyDance* (San Francisco: FatChanceBellyDance, 2005)

Nopper, Sheila. "Belly Wisdom; A New Body Politic." *Horizons.* Spring 2004. 24-46.

Mann, Susan Archer and Douglas J. Huffman. "The Decentering of Second Wave Feminism and the Rise of the Third Wave," *Science & Society,* Vol. 69, No. 1 (January 2005) 56-91.

Maira, Sunaina. "Belly Dancing: Arab-Face, Orientalist Feminism, and U.S. Empire," *American Quarterly,* Vol. 60, No. 2 (June 2008)

Marinelli, Vincenzo. "Dance of the Bee in the Harem," 1862. Oil on canvas. Museo e gallerie nazionali di Capodimonte. Photo courtesy of ARTStor digital database

Maude Allen as *Salome.* Photograph.

Mitchell, Molly. "Orientalism, the Gaze, and Representations of Femininity within American Tribal Style Belly Dance," *Sightlines* (2009) 128-154.

Pappas, Leslie A. "Shake wiggle and roll hooks new generation; women these days find they're more at ease with belly dancing," *Philadelphia Inquirer,* March 11, 2004.

Roby, Cynthia. "Professionals take the stage in belly dancing; Rakassah Festival attracts all ages and shapes, " *The San Francisco Chronicle*, March 19, 2004.

Russo, Yosheved Miriam. "The art of the (belly) dance," *The Jerusalem Post,* October 27, 2006.

Saliba, Therese. "Arab Feminism at the Millennium," Signs, Vol. 25, No. 4, Feminisms at a

Millennium (Summer, 2000). University of Chicago Press.

Shay, Anthony and Barbara Sellers-Young. "Belly Dance: Orientalism: Exoticism: Self-Exoticism," *Dance Research Journal*, Vol. 35, No. 1 (Summer, 2003) 13-37.

Taylor, Nicole. "Belly dancing seen as sisterly rather than sexy exercise," *Sydney Morning Herald,* April 13, 1989.

van Nieuwkerk, Karin. *'A Trade like Any Other;' Female Singers and Dancers in Egypt* (Austin: Univ of Texas Press, 1995)

Vincenzo Marinelli. *Dance of the Bee in the Harem* (1862). Oil on canvas. Museo e gallerie nazionali di Capodimonte. Photo courtesy of ARTStor digital database.

Yoshihara, Mari. *Embracing the East; White Women and American Orientalism* (Oxford: Oxford University Press. 2003)

Endnotes

[i] A mizmar is a wind instrument, played across the region of the Middle East at weddings and as accompaniment to belly dancing; a doumbek is a goblet shaped hand drum; zils are metal finger cymbals.

[ii] While the exact origin of the term *hootchy-kootchy* is unclear, the term was immediately used to describe the scandalous, sexualized dance from the Middle East, no matter the specific style or ethnic background of the dance or dancers.

[iii] Curtis, G.W. *Nile Notes of a Howadji* (London: Vizetelly. 1852), 88.

[iv] Buonaventura, Wendy. *Serpent of the Nile; Women and Dance in the Arab World* (New York: Interlink Books, 1998), 25.

[v] Shay, Anthony and Barbara Sellers-Young. "Belly Dance: Orientalism: Exoticism: Self-Exoticism," *Dance Research Journal*, Vol. 35, No. 1 (Summer, 2003), 22.

[vi] see Juvenal, *Satire,* from *Juvenal and Persius*, transl. G.G. Ramsay, New York: Putnam, 1924; Mas'udi, *Meadows of Gold and Mines of Gems*, transl. C. Barbier de Meynard, Paris: Societe Asiatique, 1874

[vii] Shays & Sellers-Young, 50.

[viii] Buonaventura, 65.

[ix] Mitchell, Molly. "Orientalism, the Gaze, and Representations of Femininity within American Tribal Style Belly Dance," *Sightlines* (2009), 6.

[x] Buonaventura, 101.

[xi] Buonaventura, 13.

[xii] Cheryl Ganz, 2008 p.

[xiii] Toni Bentley, *Sisters of Salome*, p. 36

[xiv] Shay & Sellers-Young, 16.

[xv] Shay & Sellers-Young 17.

[xvi] Yoshihara, 2003; Shay & Sellers-Young, 2003; Sunaina, 2008; Dox, 2006

[xvii] See Bernard Lewis, "The Question of Orientalism," New York Review of Books, June 24 1982; Lata Many and Ruth Frankenberg, "The Challenge of Orientalism," Economy and Society, vol. 14 no. 2; Bryan Turner, "From Orientalism to Global Sociology," Sociology, Nov. 1989; Sadik Jalal al-'Azm "Orientalism and Orientalism in Reverse," Khamsin, no 8, 1981; Fred

Halliday, "Orientalism and Its Critics," British Journal of Middle Eastern Studies, Vol. 20, No. 2 (1993). Halliday offers a concise critique of Said's methodology in forming his ideology, which problematizes Said's conclusions: never "does the analysis of what actually happens in these societies, as distinct from what people say and write about them, let alone the difficulties and choices of emancipatory projects, constitute the primary concern." (p. 150)

[xviii]Yoshihara, Mari. *Embracing the East; White Women and American Orientalism* (Oxford: Oxford University Press. 2003)

[xix]Yoshihara, 78.

[xx] Ibid, 78.

[xxi] Mitchell, 8. *Salome* was a one-act play written by Oscar Wilde in 1891, which tells the story of the biblical Salome, stepdaughter of Herod Antipas, who danced the *Dance of the Seven Veils* in return for the severed head of John the Baptist. The play was first performed in Paris in 1896.

[xxii] Mitchell, 9.

[xxiii] Kraus, Rachel. "Straddling the Sacred and the Secular: Creating a Spiritual Experience Through Belly Dance," Sociological Spectrum, Vol. 29, No. 5 (2009) 601.

[xxiv]Kraus,

[xxv]Sellers-Young, Barbara. "Body, Image, Identity: American Tribal Belly Dance," 278.

[xxvi] Barbara Sellers-Young, *Body, Image, Identity: American Tribal Belly Dance*; Sunaima Maira, *Belly Dancing: Arab-Face, Orientalist Feminism, and U.S. Empire*; Stavros Stavrou Karayanni, *Dancing Fear and Desire: Race, Sexuality, and Imperial Politics in Middle Eastern Dance*.

[xxvii] Maira, 329.

[xxviii] Alcoff, Linda. "Cultural Feminism versus Post-Structuralism: The Identity Crisis in Feminist Theory," Signs, Vol. 13, No. 3 (Spring, 1988) 408.

[xxix] Ibid, 409.

[xxx]Alcoff, 21.

[xxxi] Alcoff, 292.

[xxxii] Ibid, 414.

[xxxiii] Dox, Donnalee. "Dancing Around Orientalism," *The Drama Review* 50:4 (T192) Winter 2006. 55

[xxxiv] Dox, 66.

[xxxv] *Ghawazee* were a group of traveling dancers in rural Egypt, sometimes equated with gypsies. The ghawazee were banished from the capital of Cairo by Muhammad Ali for refusing to conform to the principles of Islam. Ghawazee were frequent subjects of Orientalist era paintings and literary reference.

[xxxvi] Nericcio, Carolena. *Tribal Talk; A retrospective The Voice of FatChanceBellyDance*, (San Francisco: FatChanceBellyDance, 2005), 20.

[xxxvii]Brook, James, Chris Carlsson & Nancy Peters. *Reclaiming San Francisco; History, Politics, Culture* (San Francisco: City Lights Books. 1998), 15.

[xxxviii] Brook, 20.

[xxxix] Nericcio, 20. Contrast this, for example, to the experiences of any serious student of ballet, who is under constant scrutiny to achieve perfection not only in her dance technique, but in her physique as well. Maira's research confirms, "Belly dance resonates with contemporary American feminist politics about body image and is viewed as liberating for women who are tired of conforming to the anorexic body type." (333).

[xl] Djoumahna, Kajira. "Ignorance is Bliss; An interview with Carolena Nericcio, Instructor & Director of FatChanceBellyDance of San Francisco," *Crescent Moon Magazine* (March-April 1996)

[xli]Djoumahna,, 27.

[xlii] Downey, Dennis J., Justine J. Reel, Sonya SooHoo and Sandirine Zerbib. "Body Image in Belly dance: integrating alternative norms into collective identity," *Journal of Gender Studies,* Vol. 19 No. 4 (Dec. 2010), 384.

[xliii]Mann, Susan Archer and Douglas J. Huffman. "The Decentering of Second Wave Feminism and the Rise of the Third Wave," *Science & Society,* Vol. 69, No. 1 (January 2005), 71.

[xliv]Mann,

[xlv]Mann, 74.

[xlvi]Ibid, 73.

[xlvii] Mitchell, 3.

[xliii]Mitchell, 13.

[xlix]Nericcio, 11.

[l] Kenny, 309.

[li] Kenny, 311.

[lii] Taylor, Nicole. "Belly dancing seen as sisterly rather than sexy exercise," *Sydney Morning Herald,* April 13, 1989.

[liv] Yocheved Miriam Russo. "The art of the (belly) dance," *The Jerusalem Post,* October 27, 2006.

[lv] Downey et al., 389.

Author's Bio

Robin Foster is a doctoral candidate in American Studies at Rutgers University-Newark and is Adjunct Professor of Cultural and Urban Anthropology at Seton Hall University. She danced for a blissful time with an ATS troupe in western New Jersey.

Tribes—and you...

By Paulette Rees-Denis

We live in a world of amazing diversity—assorted cultures and subcultures, mainstream and avant-garde, rich and poor (in so many ways), introverts and extroverts, online and offline communities, green juicers and biggie sizers. We have the opportunity to choose the life we desire, or at least we hope to. We strive, we thrive, we dream and we dance. We create art in whatever form speaks to and from our soul, using words, paint, food, plants, bodies. We yearn for connection with a common thread running through it. We need solitude, but we crave a gathering of like-minded folk. We desire to join a tribe.

What is a tribe?
In general, it is a group of people with a leader. In most cases, they have similar values.

A tribe can be defined as a social division of a people, in terms of common descent, territory, culture. Many **anthropologists** *used the term tribal society to refer to societies organized largely on the basis of* **kinship***. In Historical Terms it is referred to as an ethnic or ancestral division of ancient cultures. Or a tribe can be:*

a. a large number of persons, animals, etc.
b. a specific class or group of persons
c. a family, especially a large one

What can having a tribe do for you? A tribe validates your voice; the members will follow the lead and help spread their message. A tribe is like a posse, a gathering up of peeps who help you feel relevant and visible, a part of something.

In my Tribal Bellydance world, we refer to our groups, our troupes, as tribes. In the beginning days of my developing this Gypsy Caravan Tribal Bellydance (™) style, some twenty plus years ago, I decided to call this newly evolving and quickly spreading dance *Tribal Bellydance*, to reflect back on some ancient times of tribes, to honor what had come before, from tribal cultures around the world. Where villages and families would gather and play music and dance, because that is what they did (imagine no computers, phones, TVs!). To bring together the feeling of camaraderie, of the circle where everyone is accepted and important to the big picture, from the older wise folk to the babes in arms. Where folk supported each other, worked on bettering themselves, and celebrated the cycles of life, each day, and each other.

Today, who is my tribe?

My dancing tribe are predominantly women—dancers, movers, shimmiers and shakers, funky and wild, loving creative folk. We are folk who sometimes need a nod, a push, some new skills, some kind acknowledgment or a fire-startin' kick in the booty, a hug and a smile, a new workout to change it up, a sacred space to experiment and to heal. This tribe wants connection and communion, and we desire to make magic together, to raise energy to heal ourselves and each other, to feel great in our bodies, to support each other.

These Tribal dancers are global priestesses. Maidens, mothers, crones—we dance on this journey called life. We dance to connect to our goddesshood, to honor and acknowledge those who have come before, and to layout the legacy for those to come after us.

We choose to decorate and adorn ourselves with rich exotic fabrics, jangly bells, heavy amber necklaces, glittery eye shadow, feathered headdresses—just some of the accoutrements of the dance. Or maybe we just want stretchy pants and tank tops to wear while we dance away the day! We may be pierced and full on tattooed goddesses, or white uniformed 9-5er goddesses, or both.

As dancers in this style, we learn, first, how to move our bodies with the different isolated body movements. Tribal Bellydance is based on two main defining factors, one that it is a dance to be done with a group (at least two dancers but the more the merrier!), and two, that it is based on an improvisational language of moves. It is not true improvisation, as that means creating something from nothing. Here we have a structured language of moves; these dance steps become our non-verbal language. But we put them together improvisationally, and that is powerful. When I started this style, there was just one language, and now there are many dialects around the world, which is very exciting.

So how does one dance with others? They learn the moves, but they learn how to be a dancer, by not only toning and strengthening their body, which is their creative tool, like a painter uses a brush, but knowing what the body can and can't do, which could reflect age, flexibility, and skill level. One of the things that makes this dance so magnificent is that it is a dance for everyone and every body, all ages, all sizes. So body awareness is necessary, while we learn how to move all parts of the body, adding layers and various techniques. Knowing how your body works, developing muscle memory, and letting go of ego is profound for a dancer. Once you learn how to move, you can let the body go and allow your spirit to soar!

Dancing this language in an improvisational format with others means there is a leader, who puts moves together as she dances, not making up new moves, but combining known moves in the moment, and they may have one or several followers. Sometimes there are subtle cues given for certain steps, but mostly it is just being present, right then. Developing trust and confidence takes time and is empowering. This is a truly awesome creative process which can happen in a matter of weeks, or it could take years. All if that is just fine, as we learn how to dance with each other, how to lead dancers you may not know, and how to follow moves you have never seen. It is not about being perfect, or getting it correct, it is about creating together. Some are stronger leaders and some are powerful followers, although it is wonderful to learn how to do both. Each is important, as everyone in the circle is necessary to complete the whole. And each dancer makes the other dancer look incredible! No egos here, just powerful artmaking. This is what Tribal Bellydance is about.

Once you know how this works, then you can develop your conversation even further with your tribe of dancers, as your language repertoire grows, you can change up the conversation even more, switching out leaders and using various exciting formations, adding props such as veils, baskets, fans, swords, adding floor work (dancing while using levels to the floor and back up). Then of course you get to play with costuming ideas, visions of what makes your own tribe unique, what your signature moves are. That is an amazing creative process that maybe the director or instructor has the vision, desire, and skill to create. Over the many years, Gypsy Caravan Dance Company have had elaborate costumes to more simple designs and it has been fun to work with our musicians developing musical sets to go with costuming ideas and vice versa. (You can watch our documentary, *Tribal Travels, a Collage*, to see years of different costumes, performance venues, rehearsals, and interviews. This is a great source for more information on our Tribal style!)

I believe that ultimately, the dance is not about performance. It is about dancing together, whether in a studio, a living room, a backyard. Performing the dance takes another level of skill, and desire to be an entertainer. I've seen many dancers pushed into this role way too early, and that can break the dance and the dancer. Being patient and really allowing oneself to learn and develop as a dancer is a beautiful practice, and there is nothing more brilliant to watch than a dancer blooming, unfolding her or his self as this soulful creative spirit. And then if the dancer desires to go on stage when she is ready, the dance can be a true gift for the audience, and that is what I want to see as an observer—soul felt and inspired dance.

Magic is created when I dance with other dancers. It is being in the moment that allows this incredible energy and connection with another. Being present and free to move. As in a moving meditation. In my workshops and certification courses, I train dancers how to use their eyes as well as their bodies, so eventually they can dance with almost anyone from any tribe, with confidence and joy, because they can lead and follow, and because they can trust their bodies to flow while they watch with their eyes. Plus they know how to listen to the music. Understanding music, learning how to count, and allowing the music to move through you is a learned skill. Layers of knowledge goes hand in hand with layers of soul felt movement.

What does the dance do for us? It is the exhilaration of the tribal style, of dancing spontaneously together, in the moment, that moves us. Learning and allowing ourselves to move is healing on many incredible levels. Once we learn enough of the dance steps, then we connect through our soul, to ourselves and to each other, the knowing the whole body as a creative vessel and a temple of love. We dance to bleed, we dance to heal. It sets our heart on fire and our blood pumping. We dance to guide us. We dance to help us with our daily work. We dance to laugh and because it feels good.

Through the dance we can push our limits and our body, to know our body as the creative vessel, our temple of love. Because we view our bodies as we move, we see our wholeness or the parts of us that we want to work on. It builds self-acceptance as well as acceptance of all of our diversities. Forgiveness and empowered strength on our tribal journey, with the power of the tribe.

The dance helps us feel the beautiful sensual creatures that we are. And it connects us with all parts of ourselves-body, mind, spirit. Dancing is finding God, within and without, a moving meditation of different sorts. It keeps us in the moment, to be present and aware. Whether we dance alone or in a group, we can still have a tribe, and we use the skills and body awareness that we learn. I always call the improvisational format *problem solving*, and once we trust ourselves to act and move quickly and spontaneously in dance class, we can do that in our everyday life, trusting our instincts and our intuition. Tribal ideas then translate into everyday life. We can dance through our lives with power and beauty and soul.

As the Tribal Bellydance style grows and spreads, with more dialects, let us not separate the tribes but keep on spreading the love and passion of this dance, making our art, and making the world a happier place, because each of us can become a healthier and move vibrant being living in a body that is strong and creative.

Is having a tribe what you desire? Dancers, writers, motorcycle riders, business entrepreneurs, there are tribes of sorts for every genre of work and play. Sometimes you have to go in search of a tribe, and sometimes your tribe finds you. Reach out, start one, join one. Keeping your mind, spirit and body alive through community and connection, that is where it is at. Doing what you love, with passion and commitment—a tribe can help you with that. Get revved up and dance your life's dreams.

And my role, my soul purpose, well, I am the Tribal Hostess, a leader of sorts, a guide, as I gather the posses and introduce them to the dance world and to each other. As an instructor, I love to share the tools of the trade. My role is to get you up and moving and feeling and sharing. I see the relationships that are built around the dance, with each other. But still, first and most importantly, with oneself, as we travel on the tribal journey.

And we shall always dance.

Paulette Rees-Denis is an instigator and inspirator worldwide, the director of Gypsy Caravan Dance Company, and innovator of Tribal Style Bellydance. She is the author of Tribal Vision: A Celebration of Life Through Tribal Bellydance, plus eleven Tribal Technique DVDs. Lots of good Tribal goings-on, so check out her online class offerings, plus Tribal Bliss--Dance and Vision course, and the Tribal Quest Experience, and the whereabouts of her upcoming Collective Soul and Teacher Training Certification courses. Sign up on her website to get on the tribal journey. She can be found at www.paulettereesdenis.com
Email dance@gypsycaravan.us

Women's Dance in the Islamic World

By Arikah Peacock

In western eyes, when dance comes to mind it is of ballet, hip-hop, jazz, tap, or even Latin American dances such as the Salsa or the Argentinian Tango. Most, except the BellyDancer, do not think of Belly Dance, Folkloric tribal dances, or rituals. Dance in the Islamic World is just that. There are many stereotypes surrounding the people that perform the dances and the dance alone. They are often branded terms that are inappropriate such as gypsies and prostitutes. Many of the dances are shunned or looked down upon by not only the western world but some Islamic believers and it is hard to fully understand their origins and evolutions.

Islam disapproves of mixed dancing; a dance that radiates such strong erotic energy and furthers the feminine sexual force should simply not be performed in public. While acknowledging the power of the feminine, Islam sees it as a potentially disruptive factor, unless it be controlled by rules and regulations -hence the use of the veil, the segregation of the sexes, and the practice of isolation. The author of this observation is well versed in Arabic studies and ethnology. The information of this statement is not universal however it is a shared view of the members of the Islamic world. Many Islamic Women grew up dancing together. The dance was and still is performed by women for women in the Islamic World. Yet, men have folkloric dances that unfortunately go unnoticed.

Women who dance outside of the women's circle are often branded as prostitutes. The Ghawazi dancers of Egypt are known as such. Some Ghawazi are street performers but not all share their bed for pay; most dance for pay. Yet, there are those who feel they have no choice or know no other way to earn their way to food or shelter. It can be said that some are prostitutes however it would be a misconception to brand the entire dancing world as such. The Ghawazi members who have promoted themselves as prostitutes have branded the remaining members with the same type of reputation.

Some say the Ghawazi may be part of the Indo-Persian Gypsies who migrated from northern India up toward Spain and Eastern Europe. The Ghawazi, like the "Gypsies," are of non-Egyptian origin, stay apart from the rest of society, have carefully preserved their own traditions an oral history, and have their own language of obscure derivation that they speak among themselves. The correlations of these two groups are fascinating. The dance of the Ghawazi still in existence today is characterized by continuous hip shimmies from side to side, which can also be seen in classic belly dance movements.

Many women grew up with their grandmothers and mothers performing in the markets. It is taboo, forbidden, or harem to dance outside of the women's sacred circle. In our present times this exists but the western world is attempting to change their minds. The dance of the Islamic world by the western world is recognized as Belly Dance. Many of Muslim people see it as Raks Sharqi, Oriental Dance, or Dance of the East. The difference is huge. Many of the folkloric dances of Algeria and Tunisia are Raqs Shabi. Belly Dance is a melting pot of traditional dances. Raks Sharqi is the Classical Egyptian style of dance that was developed in the 1950's and introduced to the United States. The women's dance of Islam goes back to the beginning of time.

Imagine this: there was a time in history, a long time ago, when the bounce and sway of a woman's hips was considered so beautiful that they set it to music and made a dance out of it. The first dance movement of time is a simple walking gesture. Dances over time have come from watching animals, people, and other forces of nature. The first movement that women in the Islamic world learn as a child is through learning the alphabet. She draws the alif or the first letter of the Arabic alphabet which is a line. She learns that she can draw shapes with her body. The second letter of the Arabic alphabet is the Baa. The dot is the beginning. The dot begets all the other letters. The Baa is a horizontal alif with a dot underneath. Together, they will form the word father, one of the names of the Divine. When whirling or circling the pelvis you are drawing the dots origins. Dance in the Islamic world has a meaning. It is not just dancing for dancing sake.

The Guedra tribe of Morocco sees time as circular and not linear. The gestures in their dance use the flicking of their wrists and they acknowledge the four directions, elements, and time. Why does she touch her abdomen? In the East, the heart is known to be fickle and unreliable. When somebody wishes to convey true depth of affections or emotions, the way of expressing it is to say: "You are in my liver," not "You are in my heart," as we do in the west. There are about two hundred different Berber tribes in Morocco, each with its distinctive dress (especially for women), language, dance, and social customs.

The Guedra are a matriarchal Berber society. Their name means melting pot, the ritual or dance, and their tribe. The ritual of the Guedra is performed only by women and the men are veiled which is unique in the Islamic world. "Berber" does not refer to a single, unified language but serves as an umbrella term to describe a number of related linguistic varieties. In Morocco, Berber-speaking populations inhabit the mountainous regions of the Rif and the Middle Atlas in the north and center, and the High Atlas and Anti-Atlas mountains as well as the Sus Valley in the South. Another large group of Berber speakers is comprised of the Tuareg populations in the Saharan regions of Niger, Mali, Southern Algeria, and Burkina Faso.

The Guedra belong to the Blue people of the Tuareg Berber, from that part of the Sahara Desert which ranges from Mauritania into Morocco and Algeria. These people are native and inhabited the region far before the Islamic world came into North Africa. All Blue People are Tuareg, but not all Tuaregs are "blue." They are called Blue because of the indigo they use to dye their cloths and veils that they are adorned with. For the Blue people, Guedra is not merely a dance. This dance is taught in rare occasions in the United States. It is fortunate that it is beginning to be more widely understood. More sources are becoming available and the ritual itself is being learned in corners of the world.

The Guedra women of Morocco and the Kabyle women of Algeria wear their wealth as adornments on their bodies. Interestingly enough some members of the Romani people wear their wealth also with coins sewed into their clothes or on their garments. Women build up savings accounts by collecting the jewelry made from coral, local silver, and enamel. These adornments are used in many dances to make jingling sounds that ad to the presentation of the dance. It is not only a symbol of beauty but of prestige. There are many correlations between the Roma people and the people of the Islamic world. The Turkish Rom for example are Muslim. Their dances are similar throughout by way of hip movements and hand gestures.

Many dances in the Islamic world use gestures of everyday life. Many have no context to everyday life at all. Women are portrayed as putting on make-up or making cous-cous in dances. The dances can be theatrical or traditional. Men and women in Algeria and Tunisia will dance with a jar on their head to show their talents of balancing. The dance Raqs Shabi presents many side to side movements of the hips performed by both men and women. Men dance with other props such as swords or guns. Dancing on one leg is common in the men's dances. Many of the regions have a version of a musket dance. Members of the Sufi brotherhood are descendants of slaves from West Africa. The dances they perform are called Banga from Nefta.

Not every Muslim is a radical and not every dancer is a prostitute. This is not to say that this does not exist, however it is narrow-minded to believe that this is the only case. The western world has been exposed to media that paints an unnecessary picture of the Islamic world. News of the opposing side in a war is only going to show negative issues of their opponent. This, alone, can askew the views of the public. Take televisions shows for an example such as *I dream of Jeannie* with her Turkish stylized hat and her bare belly showing. Using with the inaccurate term, "Gypsy", leads the American thinker to visualize a crystal ball reading by the well-known Professor Marvel in the Wizard of Oz. One may assume it is the old wicked witch who has a huge nose ring, tarot cards, and her campfire. She may put a spell on you and is mesmerizing. It is a fantasy misnomer that gives the wrong impression of this term in the westerners mind.

The "Gypsy" is often depicted in one's mind to be one who is unclean, an outsider, an outcast, as well as an even more romantic stereotype. The movie *Gypsy Lee Rose* gives another fantasy idea of who these people may be. These are misconceptions. For a note, the term "Gypsy" is offensive by many, almost to the majority of their culture. These people, overall, agree to be called a different name according to the dialect in which they speak and/or the traditions they uphold. For example, a vast majority want to be called the Roma/ Rroma, Romani/ Romany, or Rromani/Rromany. Not to mention other groups which are the Sinti, the Banjara, the Gitano, the Nawar and Ghawazee/Ghawazi. Europeans mislabeled them as "Gypsies" because they were believed to have come from Egypt. (Djoumahna, Belly Dance -In Brief 2000) To the uneducated westerner the term "Gypsy" is widely accepted and misunderstood. It is time to create awareness. If a word to describe a racial, ethnic, or cultural group is offensive in naming the particular group, one should not use it.

It is common for the westerner to call any tribal member a "gypsy" or a "genie" just due to these television programs or fantasy ideals one creates. This has no reality base to it. However in Algeria a Madak tribesman, told Thomas J. Abercrombie, writer of an article for National Geographic, "Kel Asuf!" he said: "Genies!" Abercrombie replies, "They haunt the plateau. Most were friendly genies, he had assured me, but around his neck he wore three powerful amulets just in case." References to genies are noted in the stories and movies *Aladdin*. Here, the characters are depicted as wearing pantaloons and females in nothing but a decorated bra with cartoonish imagery of belly dancing. This creates a misnomer as to what dance really is in the Islamic world.

A group of wanderers are known to have left out of Ancient North India in the 11th century.(Djoumahna, Belly Dance -In Brief 2000) These people are known to have left India due to the spreading of Islam and the raids led by Mohammed of Ghazni. Mohammed of Ghazni is the initiator in spreading Islam into Northern India. These are the people that come to be known as the "Gypsies." This is the beginning of the nomadic culture of these people and what will become the future in and of their migration. Their migration spread across the pathways of Pakistan, Persia, as some spread their travels into North Africa and some went into Europe. These groups began to divide here. Both divisions ended up meeting back in Spain and into the United Kingdom as well as the United States.

Many of these people did not travel on and settled in the said areas. The Roma people are diverse because they pick up dances, culture, and religion around the people and culture that they have assimilated into. They are a group that some debate does not even exist as an ethnic group partially because they have evolved from Indian people to being mixed with whatever ethnic group they have been surrounded by. It is taboo or harem for them to marry outside of their own group yet many have done so. It is noticed in the features of the people even by the skin color. The Romani people in the United Kingdom are much lighter than those throughout the Middle East.

Once any group begins to migrate out of their homeland their ways and traditions are more difficult to keep pure and true. Cultures influence other cultures and the group will pick up new ways and ideas along their travels. These people have been inspired by dances along their way. Dance in the Islamic world has been shaped by local tribes throughout as well as the tinkers and travelers of the Romany people who are misnamed "gypsies." Many Romany people are Muslim. However, in leaving India, they took with them their rich Hindu heritage. This became more and more lost over time yet is still more prominent in the Banjara tribe who are found in Southern India. The exact dates of these groups in many cases are not known. The Banjara left Northern India in the 17th century during the regime of the Mughals.

The date of the Gypsies first appearance in England is unknown.(Journal of the Gypsy Lore Society Vol. 1 1889) The Gitanos arrived in Spain during the 15th century. Everywhere these groups went they were looked down upon, persecuted, and/or expelled from their camp or residence. One escape for these people was dance. At one time Spain was occupied by Islamic forces and the influence of the Islamic world echoed through Romany culture and Romany culture through the Islamic world. These groups have inspired Eastern dance since the beginning of time. Dance of the Islamic world is spread not only by locals but the Romani people who have travelled, migrated, or settled in these regions so they are acknowledged as dancers of the Islamic world.

The Ouled Nail of Algeria, another group of people of mysterious origins, have kept themselves apart and maintained their ancient traditions much like the Ghawazi and the Roma. These unveiled public dancers of the Sahara Djurdjura were famous for their jeweled crown, or zeriref, as far back as the 6th century B.C.E. These headdresses are adorned with coins and stones that illuminate the dance. These dancers portray what the western world would associate with Belly Dance. Beginning slowly, in a stationary position, the dancer first rolls her belly in a circular movement.

Many times in the Middle East and North Africa women must earn their dowries. At times it is through dance. After women earn their dowries by their dance, which in no way affects their reputation at home, they return to their village to marry and live according to the Muslim society that surrounds them. This is not the case for all Islamic world dancers. Within the Arabs of the Sinai peninsula, girls sometimes achieve a reputation of purity in proportion to her tears and her struggles of resistance on her marriage day. These girls do not all need to dance for the husband to be but it can be required. This is just a small hint of the trouble that girls endure in the Islamic world and the sensitive issues that can arise alongside of dance.

The dances range from being quite colorful and loud to soft and gentle. The folkloric tribal dances are for community and ritual such as celebrating the harvest by the Fellahein people of Egypt or the Healing Ritual of the Guedra. A universal idea throughout the world is using the core or the belly to enhance the dance. This is seen throughout ballet and other western dances as well. The folkloric dances are being lost over time. This is unfortunate because it is a part of history that may be lost forever or extinct. The importance of the dance in the modern world is less emphasized. It should be studied and documented through film and other media.

Awareness can be created through research of the dance to tell the story of the people and their culture. Dance is important because it helps to unite people, express oneself through non-verbal communication, to be healthy, and to teach through imagery. Dance in and of the Islamic world should be accepted and taught alongside of other dance styles. Some of the dance costumes require more fabric than what a ballet costume would. For whatever reason people have to discriminate against the performers of the Islamic world is unfair. The dance and the performers of the dance should be respected and found important. If this were truth then the importance of determining the origin of the people who perform the dances would teach people more about the culture in order to respect them and their culture.

Dance in the Islamic world is not overall respected. It is widely discriminated against even as far as into the United States. It is not always taught in the University where the other dance styles are thankfully still taught. The origins of the performers are unclear with debate upon to where exactly the Ghawazi, Roma, and others are from. They are widely persecuted or shunned. However, they are jacks of many trades in which some are dancers. This is key to understanding this sub-group of people. The dance is their expression. The dance is their outlet or even their wealth and reputation which is not always a negative. Gratefully, as Belly Dance and forms of folkloric dancing grow around the world, appreciation can set in for people to be who they are without persecution.

[1]Rosina-Fawzia Al-Rawi., *Grandmother's Secrets* (Interlink books: 1999), 43
[2]Iris Stewart., *Sacred Woman, Sacred Dance (Inner Traditions: 2000)*, :88
[3]Ibid., 88
[4]Carolena Nericcio., quote with her permission
[5]Rosina-Fawzia Al-Rawi., *Grandmother's Secrets* (Interlink books: 1999), 5

[6]Ibid., 5

[7]Carolina Dinicu., *Guedra: Spreading Soul's Love and Peace to the Best of the Heart* (Habibi: 1993), 5

[8]Ibid., 4

[9]Jane E. Goodman., *Berber Culture on the World Stage* (Indiana University Press: 2005), 6

[10]Carolina Dinicu., *Guedra: Spreading Soul's Love and Peace to the Best of the Heart* (Habibi: 1993), 5

[11]Douchan Gersi., *Faces in the Smoke* (Jeremy P. Tarcher, Inc: 1991), 69

[12]Carolina Dinicu., *Guedra: Spreading Soul's Love and Peace to the Best of the Heart* (Habibi: 1993), 4

[13]Thomas J. Abercrombie., *Algeria After a Decade of Freedom* (National Geographic: 1973), 217

[14]Kajira Djoumahna., *Belly Dance- In Brief* (Backbeat Press: 2000), 10

[15]Thomas J. Abercrombie., *Algeria After a Decade of Freedom* (National Geographic: 1973), 217

[16]Kajira Djoumahna., *Belly Dance- In Brief* (Backbeat Press: 2000), 10

[17]Journal of the Gypsy Lore Society (1889) 1

[18]Iris Stewart., *Sacred Woman, Sacred Dance (Inner Traditions: 2000),* :88

[19]Ibid., 88

[20]Ibid., 88

ARIKAH PEACOCK'S BIO

Arikah Peacock has been teaching Belly Dance in her Midwest community for 13 years. She is certified by Kajira Djoumahna in the BlackSheep BellyDance format as a Level 3 teacher and is a recognized Satellite School. She is certified by Carolena Nericcio in the FatChance BellyDance® format and is a recognized Sister Studio®. She is certified as a Reiki Master Teacher, a Health Care Practitioner, and a Zumba® Instructor. Arikah has a BA in History where she specialized in Romani culture and Dance in the Middle Eastern World. She has published articles in Belly Dance periodicals such as *Jareeda* and *Zaghareet!*. She teaches at her local YMCA as a prenatal dance and yoga instructor, a Kundalini and Hatha yoga instructor, a Silver Sneaker® teacher, and dance instructor. She teaches dance and yoga at her local community college as well as Millikin University's gym. She offers Belly Dance for a college credit too! Arikah is the creative director of Ees'aBella BellyDance and a proud member of BlackSheep BellyDance and Daughters of the Dance. Arikah and Ees'aBella are sponsors and hosts of an annual event called Bellies for Bellies featuring different styles of Belly Dance where proceeds go to a local food pantry and By Grace Orphan and Disabled Centre in Nairobi, Kenya where Arikah has done volunteer work with the children. Arikah co-owns Healing Arts Boutique and Studio where she teaches movement classes, offers Body Art such as Body Piercings, Henna, and Hair Adornments. She reads tarot and practices massage therapy.

www.eesabellabellydance.com
PeacockBell@yahoo.com

The Salimpour Influence on American Belly Dance

by V. Totten

Jamila Salimpour was born in New York City in 1926. She grew up hearing her father's stories of the dancers he saw in North Africa when he was in the Sicilian Navy. Jamila joined the Ringling Brothers and Barnum Baily circus at the age of sixteen. At nineteen, she moved to Los Angeles where she became connected to a diverse but close-knit group of Middle Eastern immigrants. With this new community, she once again became engrossed with Middle Eastern dance. As there were no teachers of the dance, she researched and learned what she could by watching, listening, and reading. Few if any clubs on the West Coast had belly dancing at that time, so Jamila began by performing mostly for woman-only groups. She also taught off and on to small groups of students. By her late 20s, when belly dancers were now allowed and featured in the clubs, Jamila performed regularly in restaurants and nightclubs.

Around 1960, Jamila was recruited to perform in San Francisco where she eventually settled permanently. There she owned part of a night club and danced full-time until she married at the beginning of 1966. After marriage, Jamila's husband forbade her from dancing. She immediately got pregnant, and Suhaila was born later that year. Jamila sold her half of the nightclub and taught belly dance to bring in money to the family.

In 1968, Jamila's Bal Anat first debuted at the Renaissance Pleasure Faire featuring folkloric and fantasy dancers, with the authentic displayed right alongside hokum. Jamila's dance format technique and Bal Anat presentation began the tribal movement and stylization that would soon take root in the belly dance community.

1966 to about 1984 is considered Jamila's greatest period of teaching. She turned 40 in 1966, so she was a mature woman who had already been involved in the dance for 20 years. She had seen the original Egyptian movies imported from Egypt within a year of their Cairo debuts. She had connections that gave her the latest music recordings and trends from the Middle East. She was present and watching as the dance arrived and grew on the West Coast. And she, herself, played a significant role in how the dance was taught. She observed elements from various dancers and codified the steps into families. She added structure and timing. Her famous finger cymbal method included over 44 patterns. By 1980, her format was documented in a manual and video tape series, including several important additions and concepts from Suhaila.

Born in 1966, Suhaila grew up around her mother's classes. Jamila did not instruct Suhaila directly. Instead, Suhaila picked up her mother's format by sitting and observing the classes when she was a small child. Jamila enrolled Suhaila in ballet, jazz, and tap at a very early age, so Suhaila learned Western dance technique and developed a Western bodyline. Simultaneously, she was cataloguing her mother's format in her head by watching her mother teach. Inevitably, Suhaila began to fuse and overlay what she was learning as a young child. She layered her mother's iconic format onto a well-developed Western posture, allowing for even more range. By the age of nine, Suhaila was teaching with her mother. By the age of twelve, Suhaila was teaching by herself and traveling out-of-state to teach Salimpour format workshops by herself.

But Suhaila was also continuing to develop as a dancer. She saw the gaps in her mother's format and wanted to find a way to further expand the movement vocabulary and possibilities. She began to write and document her own format and way of explaining the dance that expanded the format exponentially. Dancers before had talked about breaking down certain moves and maybe a few isolations. But Suhaila was the first to break down all movements completely to reintegrate as either percussive or fluid movements. She began seeing all forms of dance and movement differently by exploring how they could be orientalized and how to represent different stylizations within oriental dance. As a young teenager, she watched and studied popping and locking, the latest urban dance craze, being developed and evolved right in San Francisco. She brought this additional isolation work into the dance throughout her middle and high school years.

The music imported from the Middle East began changing, as well. In the 1970s and 1980s, complex and layered compositions became more common. In some cases, composers were creating for dancers instead of singers. Jamila and Suhaila were riveted by the changes in the music and were eager to properly represent the new sound. With Suhaila's training, the two collaborated on choreographing several signature pieces including Joumana, Maharjan, and Hayati.

Breaking down and isolating movements was not anything new. Many belly dancers had their one signature move or two that called for a break or isolation of some sort. Jazz and modern dancers experimented with isolating movements. Poppers and lockers were breaking down any body movements possible. Suhaila, herself, identified and then developed a formal method to separate the glute muscles from the leg muscles for hip work; this, alone, revolutionized how belly dance was taught.

What Suhaila did for belly dance was to take the overall concept of isolations and breaks and apply it to ALL (not just a few) belly dance movements with an orientalized approach. In the late 1970s, Suhaila added many isolations (pelvic locks, chest locks, interior hip squares, etc.) to her mother's format; these were included in Jamila's *Danse Orientale* manual published in 1978. She taught dance by identifying specific muscles that were the primary force behind each movement. For the first time, belly dancers were being taught to move from the inside out by moving their muscles. She applied timing, downbeat, and directional  options. Her method also provided a means to teach and train layering. Suhaila's method allowed for more layering, thereby giving students greater capacity for movement, expression, and individuality. Now, all dancers could learn all isolation possibilities and all layering options as a matter of course and regular training.

Jamila is called the mother of American tribal belly dance because of the significant influence of her technique as applied to her Bal Anat troupe and presentation. Equally significant are Suhaila's influences to tribal fusion. Suhaila was the first to bring in the breaks, isolations, and layering that are now commonplace elements of tribal fusion belly dance and, in fact, many stylizations of belly dance today.

By the time Suhaila graduated high school in 1985, Suhaila had her format mostly outlined as she had been teaching and developing it for nearly ten years. She spent the next decade performing in the night clubs (prestigious Byblos in Los Angeles and in the Middle East). During that time, she put both her mother's and her own format to the test, continuing to fine-tune and develop. After retiring from her night club career, Suhaila began, and continues today, to teach, choreograph, and direct fulltime in addition to her theater performances (solo and group). In 1996 she created the Suhaila Dance Company. In 1999, Suhaila launched the Suhaila certification program and took over direction of Bal Anat. In 2009, she launched the Jamila Salimpour certification program.

Suhaila's format would not exist without Jamila's. Jamila's format is belly dance history, giving an outline of the basic step families with classic Egyptian stylization. Although a full and solid format on its own, Jamila's format was expanded and enriched by the introduction of elements from Suhaila. Then, as she taught her mother's format, Suhaila wanted options to expand beyond the basic steps and stylization. She created her own format that encompassed her mother's step families but allowed for limitless options, layers, and stylizations. Both Jamila's format and Suhaila's format have transformed how belly dance is analyzed and taught today.

Salimpour Biographies

Jamila Salimpour and Suhaila Salimpour are a family dynasty in American belly dance. Jamila (born 1926) is the Matriarch of Belly Dance in the United States and the Mother of Tribal Belly dance. Inspired by the great dancers of Egypt's Golden Era, she was a cabaret dancer in the early West Coast clubs of the United States. She applied the same technique to her Bal Anat troupe (a gathering of many tribes) but with different stylization and costuming to different music to achieve a different sentiment. She was the first to develop and codify a belly dance format, and she created a finger cymbal method including over 44 patterns.

Suhaila Salimpour (born 1966) grew up with her mother's format and Bal Anat while learning Western dance; she spent a decade performing in prestigious night clubs with live bands in the Middle East and Los Angeles. In 1996, she began the Suhaila Dance Company. In 1999, she took over direction of Bal Anat and launched the Suhaila Salimpour Belly Dance certification program, the most extensive and thorough belly dance curriculum available. She launched the Jamila Salimpour Belly dance certification program in 2007 to further augment and expand the Salimpour School. Her own format, first developed in 1978 has revolutionized the way that belly dance is understood and taught today.

More information about the Salimpour family and their education materials are available at SuhailaInternational.com.

Writer Biography

V. Totten has been documenting the Salimpour family and their contributions to belly dance since 2000. She edited *The New Danse Orientale* (rewrite of Jamila's format) published in 2013; she edited *Jamila's Article Book: Selections of Jamila Salimpour's Articles Published in Habibi Magazine, 1974-1988* published in 2013. Currently, she is editing *The Suhaila Salimpour Belly Dance Format* manual and *The Salimpour Format Study Guide*, both set for publication in 2014.

THE BINDI

By Halima

"A woman's beauty is multiplied 1,000 times when she wears a bindi" – Hindu Proverb

Bindis are making a fashion statement everywhere besides the dance community. We have all been fascinated with them even before they became so popular in our country. We have heard rumors of what they are suppose to signify; caste system, religion, etc. But what we really cared the most about was the beauty and the significance of something exotic; after all women everywhere love the idea of beauty in whatever form.

Have you ever wondered why the women of India wear the little red dot on their forehead? Many people think that it has something to do with the caste system of India. Bindis are such a part of India's heritage and culture but they have absolutely nothing to do with the caste system.

Pronounced Bin Dee, the word bindi is derived from the Sanskrit word bindu, which means "drop." There are two common meanings of bindi throughout India. The first is tied to Hindu religion and the second is a social symbol. Many believe it is suppose to be representative of the mystic third eye and becomes the central point of the base of creation. The area between the eyebrows (where the bindi is placed) is said to be the sixth chakra, Agni, the seat of "concealed wisdom." According to the followers of Tantrism, this chakra is the exit point for kundalini energy. The bindi is said to retain energy and strengthen concentration. It is also said to protect against demons or bad luck. Therefore, the traditional red dot) often made with tikka powder or vermillion) can be seen on men and women. When visiting a temple, it is common for the priest to mark men, women, and children using his finger.

The second historical and cultural significance of bindi is as a social symbol very similar to western wedding bands. Bindi were worn by married women in North India in the form of a little red dot. Red was chosen because the color was supposed to bring good fortune into the home of the bride. The red mark made the bride the preserver of the family's honor and welfare. Over time, they also became a fashion accessory and changed in shape and colors.

In the past few decades, not only married women have taken up this beautiful accessory. Girls of all ages enjoy wearing a variety of styles and colors. Today, these little gems are often matched with the color clothing a person is wear and is a must with sari, sares, salwar kameez or other Indian dress. It is also used as body art as well as an accessory to belly dance and ethnic dance. They come with a sticker like back that allows you to place the bindi securely.Traditionally bindi is a dot of red color applied in the center of the forehead close to the eyebrows, but it can also consist of a sign or piece of jewelry worn at this location.

In addition to the bindi, in India, a vermilion mark in the parting of the hair just above the forehead is worn by married women as a symbol of their married status. During North Indian marriage ceremonies, the groom applies indoor on the parting in the bride's hair.

Here are other names that bindis are known by:

Pottu in Tamil and Malayalam

Tilak in Hindi

Bottu or Tilakam in Kannada

Teep (meaning "a pressing") in Bengali

Nande is a term erroneously used to describe the bindi in Malaysia. It may contain pejorative connotations although not in most cases.

Sometimes the terms sindoor, krumkum, or kasturi are used, by reference to the material used to make the mark

In modern times, the bindi has become a decorative item and is worn by unmarried as well as non-Hindu women India, Bangladesh and other countries of South Asia. It is no longer restricted in color or shape. Self-adhesive bindis (also known as sticker bindis) are available as well. They are usually made of felt or thin metal and come with an adhesive on one side. These are simple to apply and are disposable substitutes for older tilak bindis. Sticker bindis come in many colors, designs, materials, and sizes. Fancy sticker bindis may be decorated with sequins, glass beads, or rhinestones for extra dazzle.

Bindis are worn as a style statement by such international celebrities such as Gwen Stefani, Shakira, Madonna, Nelly Furtado and Shania Twain to mention a few. So be creative and add some bindis to your fashion accessories.

Raqs in Egypt

By Shira

Although the origins of *raqs* (belly dance) are lost in time, it is possible to explore more recent history in the countries of origin.

Most of the information available in English about the history of *raqs* in Egypt can be traced to European traveler's tales. The earliest of these were written by individuals who accompanied Napoleon Bonaparte's army when it invaded Egypt in 1798. This invasion sparked a strong European interest in Egypt, leading to the rise of tourism, colonial occupation, archeology expeditions, business ventures, and more over the centuries that followed.

Before Europeans began traveling to Egypt in large numbers, there were two primary classes of *raqs* performers. The *Awalim* were educated women who performed privately in the homes of upper-class Egyptians to entertain the women of the harem. In addition to dancing, they sang and recited poetry. Men of the household might be allowed to hear the *Awalim* singing, but not to see them dance. The other class was the *Ghawazee*, who danced more publicly, including performances at outdoor events such as *moulids* (saints' day festivals) and lower-class weddings.

In the 1830's, then-Viceroy of Egypt Mohamed Ali banished the dancers of Cairo to Upper Egypt. Many congregated at Esna, others settled in other communities. For a time, certain *Awalim* were able to remain in Cairo thanks to the patronage of their upper-class clientele, but eventually they too were forced to relocate south. The women remained in Upper Egypt for approximately 3 decades, finally allowed to return to Cairo in the 1860's after Mohamed Ali had died and one of his descendants took his place as Viceroy.

Following this return of the dancers to Cairo, a dancer named Shooq soon rose to prominence and became known as the first dancer viewed as respectable enough to perform for the upper classes, and she was the only dancer permitted to perform at parties hosted by the Viceroy. She was invited to perform at the grand opening of the Suez Canal.

Other dancers soon achieved prominence of their own. Among these were:

◻ Shafiqa el-Koptiyya, who left her family to work with Shooq in the 1870's and continued dancing into the 20th century.
◻ Salem, said by some to have been the most famous Turkish *almeh* in Egypt of the 19th century [10]
◻ Bamba Kashar, who left her family to work with Salem in the late 1870's and later went on to be the first Egyptian dancer ever to be featured in a motion picture, the 1927 silent film *Leyla*. [11]

[8] "Changing Images and Shifting Identities: Female Performers in Egypt", an essay in *Moving History / Dancing Cultures*. By Karin Van Nieuwkerk. Page 137.

[9] "الشمبانيا خيولها شربت التي الراقصة ...القبطية شفيقة". Published in *Kawakeb* magazine, 1955, reprinted at http://www.bostah.com, accessed January 30, 2014. Translation by Priscilla Adum published as "Shafiqa el-Koptiyya: The Dancer Whose Horses Drank Champagne" at http://www.shira.net/about/shafiqa-horses.htm, accessed January 30, 2014.
[10] "Bamba Kashar: A Legend of Raqs Sharqi". Originally published by Al Kahira in Arabic at http://www.alkaheranews.com/details.php?pId=17&aId=3358, accessed October, 2012. Translation by Priscilla Adum published at http://www.shira.net/about/bamba-kashar-alkahira.htm, accessed January 30, 2014.
[11] Ibid.

Around the 1880's, a new type of business began to appear in Cairo – entertainment clubs that featured a variety of acts, including music, dance, acrobatics, plays, and more. One neighborhood known for these clubs was that of Ezbekiya Garden. Another was the nearby street Emad Ad-Din. The word *sala* (plural *salat*) was often used to describe these music halls.

One of the more prominent *salat*, El Dorado, featured performances by Shafiqa el-Koptiyya. She would go into a backbend balancing a tray of four juice glasses with liquid on her abdomen, balancing a candelabrum with lit candles on her forehead, and wearing *sagat* (finger cymbals) on her hands. Shafiqa became so popular that when she entered the stage, wealthy patrons would throw gold coins at her feet, which were picked up by three of her employees. Shafiqa's spectacular success sparked many legends about her – one story is that she gilded the heels of her shoes in gold. Another tells that one of her admirers appreciated Shafiqa so much that he ordered bottles of champagne to be opened and offered to her horses to drink.

In the 1890's, *raqs al-shamadan* arose as a specialty dance, and rapidly became a tradition associated with weddings of the nobility. Photos of Egyptian dancers appearing in the Rue de Caire attraction at the Exposition Universelle in Paris in 1889 do not show any candelabra in use, nor do photos of the dancers who performed in the United States at the Columbia Exposition in Chicago in 1893. Therefore it is reasonable to conclude that the use of the *shamadan* arose after 1893, because the dancers most likely would have brought their candelabra along to the U.S. if they were using them as of that time. Photos of the dancers who performed at the next Parisian Exposition Universelle in 1900 show candelabra, so this would suggest that the *shamadan* came into usage between 1893 and 1900. Zouba el-Klobatiyya told interviewer Yousef el-Sherif that she was the first to dance with a brass *shamadan* that weighed 10 kilograms (22 pounds).

According to the Egyptian dancer Nadia Hamdi who was famed for her *shamadan* performances in the latter 20th century, Zouba el-Klobatiyya and Shafiqa el-Koptiyya were the reputed originators of the specialty. Nadia's own great-aunt Najia el Eskandrani and grandmother Dawlett both learned to use the *shamadan* from these two.

The sala business continued to thrive into the early 20th century, setting the stage for a business-savvy woman named Badia Masabni to appear on the scene. Badia was an entertainer from Syria who had also lived and worked in the music hall scene in Lebanon. On November 4, 1926, she opened her first venue in Egypt, which she called Sala Badia, in the Emad Ad Din district of Cairo. The newspaper advertisement announcing the grand opening (shown in this image) introduced the entertainment lineup, which included Badia herself singing and dancing, singing by Gamil Azit, and live music played by a 4-piece orchestra consisting of ney, kanoun, oud, and violin. As noted above, this neighborhood already featured a thriving entertainment scene by the time Badia opened her own business there.

[12] "From Café Chantant to Casino Opera." By Heather D. Ward ("Nisaa of St. Louis"). Published at http://www.gildedserpent.com/cms/2013/01/10/from-cafe-chantant-to-casino-opera/#axzz2rxCiOqQh on January 10, 2013, accessed January 31, 2014.

[13] "الشمبانيا خيولها شربت التي الراقصة ...القبطية شفيقة" Published in *Kawakeb* magazine, 1955, reprinted at http://www.bostah.com, accessed January 30, 2014. Translation by Priscilla Adum published as "Shafiqa el-Koptiyya: The Dancer Whose Horses Drank Champagne" at http://www.shira.net/about/shafiqa-horses.htm, accessed January 30, 2014.

[14] "Yousef el Sherif Discusses Zouba el-Klobatiyya." Originally published by *Al Masri Al Youm* on May 2, 2009. Translation by Priscilla Adum published at http://www.shira.net/about/zouba-el-klobatiyya.htm, accessed January 30, 2014.

[15] "Nadia Hamdi: Giving Joy to the Heart and the Eyes." By Morocco. Published in *Habibi* Volume 15, Number 2 (Spring 1996).

[16] Advertisement announcing grand opening for Sala Badia. Published in *Al Ahram*, November 4, 1926. From the private collection of Priscilla Adum.

As Badia Masabni's business became established, the entertainment she offered began to expand to include monologuists (stand-up comedians), Vaudeville-style musical theater skits, and other entertainers. The first dancer Badia hired was Afranza Hanem from Turkey. At the time, Afranza Hanem was already quite well-known in the former Ottoman empire. For weeks prior to her March 31, 1927 debut at Sala Badia, announcements were made in the newspaper that Afranza was on her way to Egypt. Badia's personal dance performances were not necessarily what we would think of as Oriental dance – often, her performances were either dance styles popular on the Vaudeville circuit, such as the Charleston, or her own innovations such as "the body dance," "the peacock dance," "the gazelle dance," "the village dance," etc.

The next year, Badia built on her success by expanding to a new location. On June 16, 1928, Badia opened a seasonal establishment in Alexandria, also called Sala Badia, to serve the Egyptians who summered at the seaside, featuring Afranza Hanem as the star performer. The newspaper advertisement announcing the Alexandria club's opening described Sala Badia as "the classiest place for families to get together and listen to *tarab*, promoting the famous singer Fathya Ahmed, Afranza Hanem, and herself as star performers. The ad described Badia as "dancing artistic dance and performing [comedy] monologues." At the end of the summer, the club closed as planned, and Badia returned her attention to the Cairo area.

In the 1930's Badia Masabni brought several new artists to work with her. In 1933, when another sala owner Soad Mahasen closed her club and returned to Lebanon, Badia hired one of her dancers, a promising young woman named Taheya Mohamed. At this time, the U.S. motion picture *Flying Down to Rio* became popular around the world, including Egypt, and featured the first-ever on-screen pairing of Fred Astaire and Ginger Rogers as dance partners doing a dance called "the carioca" to a song also called "Carioca." Soon after, young Taheya Mohamed appeared as a minor character in the Egyptian motion picture *Dr. Farhat* in which she performed a playful *shaabi* dance to the song "Carioca," and soon she had picked up the nickname Taheya Carioca, which stuck. She became known for performing the Carioca at Badia's clubs.

Sometime during the 1930's, Badia Masabni invented a new genre of dance which she dubbed *raqs sharqi*, which is Arabic for "dance of the East" or "Oriental dance." In a 1966 interview, Badia told Leyla Rostum she created it by combining traditional Egyptian hip-based dancing with Turkish, Persian, and Latin dance.

In 1940, Badia Masabni decided to move her business from the Emad ad-Din district to Opera Square. The old neighborhood had been declining, and Badia sought to reach a more upscale clientele. This marked the opening of her most famous night spot of all, the Casino Opera. The Casino Opera was large and luxurious, featuring the first circular stage in Egypt. Its clientele included the elite families of Egypt, including King Farouk. The stage of the Casino Opera featured legendary Egyptian entertainers, including dancers Taheya Carioca, Samia Gamal, and Hekhmet Fahmy; comedian Ismail Yassin; singer Farid al-Atrache, and many more.

Of all the Egyptian dance stars of the 20th century, Taheya Carioca is widely acclaimed even today as one of the greatest. Badia Masabni said in an interview, "Taheya's dance was *sharqi* (Oriental) more than any of them." Taheya Carioca started her career as a dancer, headlining at Badia's clubs, but also went on to international popularity appearing in Egyptian motion pictures. At first, Taheya was featured in dancing roles, but her talents as an actress were quickly recognized, and she continued to be featured in dramatic roles even after her retirement from dancing in the 1950's. Taheya was the only dancer to ever perform onstage with Oum Kalthoum as she sang. When Taheya died in 1999, she became the first dancer to be honored with a public funeral procession. Her obituary in the New York Times reported that she had 14 different husbands and once slapped King Farouk when he slipped an ice cube down her dress.

[17] "The Lady and Her Clubs." By Priscilla Adum. Published at http://www.shira.net/about/badia-lady-and-clubs.htm, accessed February 1, 2014.
[18] Ibid.
[19] Ibid.
[20] Badia Masabni in an interview conducted by Leyla Rostum for the Lebanese television show *Negoum 3ala El Ard*. 1966. Transcribed and translated by Priscilla Adum, published at http://www.shira.net/about/badia-interview-1966.htm, accessed February 1, 2014.
[21] Ibid.

Samia Gamal came to work for Badia Masabni in approximately 1940. Samia aspired to become a famous dancer, as famous as Taheya Carioca. She hired dance instructor Isaac Dickson, who created some of the choreography featured at Badia Masabni's club, to teach her how to dance. When she performed her very first solo at Casino Opera, the audience booed her off the stage, demanding that Taheya Carioca come out to dance instead. Rather than let this episode kill her dreams, Samia returned to her studies, and eventually became a major dance star in her own right. In 1949, Egypt's King Farouk named her the National Dancer of Egypt. Samia appeared in her first motion picture in a minor role in 1943, and her film career rose rapidly as a result of a series of six pictures she made with co-star Farid al-Atrache from 1947 through 1952. She went on to appear in over 40 movies altogether.

Many other dancers launched their careers from Badia Masabni's clubs, including Hoda Shams Eddine, Ketty, and Hagar Hamdi. Badia sold the Casino Opera in 1950 and moved to Lebanon for her retirement years.

Often referred to as "Hollywood on the Nile," Egypt's motion picture industry was the first to arise in the Arabic-speaking world, and in the decades that followed it retained its position of dominance. The first musicals appeared in the 1930's, and many of these included scenes featuring *raqs* performances. Because of Egypt's industry dominance, its films were distributed throughout the Arab world, and its dancers became international stars. Consequently, the Egyptian style of *raqs* performance became popular as an art form throughout the Arab world and remains so today.

[22] "Tahia Carioca, 79, Dies; A Renowned Belly Dancer." By Douglas Martin. *New York Times*, September 22, 1999.
[23] "Samia Gamal, a Dancer Who Believes That Middle Ground is Best!" By Fouad Moawad. Kawakeb Magazine, 1968. Republished in 2010 at http://www.shira.net/about/Interview-samia-gamal-1968-kawakeb.htm, accessed February 1, 2014. Translated by Priscilla Adum, published at http://www.shira.net/about/Interview-samia-gamal-1968-kawakeb.htm, accessed February 1, 2014.

Shira is known worldwide for her work as a researcher, author, lecturer, and publisher of information on Middle Eastern dance, music, and culture. She has been interviewed by the New York Times and Wall Street Journal for stories on Middle Eastern dance. Her web site, www.shira.net, is the most comprehensive and most linked-to Oriental dance Internet resource in the world. For continuing education, Shira has traveled three times to Turkey, nine times to Egypt, and once to Morocco. Photo by Kaylyn Hoskins of Solon, Iowa.

Dancer-Made: The World of 70's Costuming

by Jenza (Suzanne McNeil)

In the 1960's, a profound change in our cultural consciousness began to affect the face of Belly Dance in our country. The era of the Flower Child brought new enthusiastic focus on other cultures, their dances and folk arts of all kinds. By the 70's the Belly Dance became mainstream in this country; and for the first time, was the hobby of the average housewife. In turn, the ethnic needle arts from around the world especially the Middle East were expressed and worn in everyday clothing in America. Our Belly Dance costuming, influenced by these changes blossomed with new creativity.

As a beginning student in late 1974, I enthusiastically immersed myself into the seemingly endless creativity that Belly Dance and it's costuming afforded. I had just stepped into a world just as colorful and exciting as the most psychedelic art of my generation.

Everything was self-made and very few stores existed for costuming. The few stores we had were stocked with items from local designers. Mass production did not exist.

There were two genres of costuming: folk and cabaret; but crossover designs were common. In fact, until the late 1970's we all wore the more earthy styles from time to time on the cabaret stage.

We all had the same obsession with seeking out and pouring over every book we could find on the needle arts and fabric types of the Middle East, India, and the Asia.

Our first costume almost always consisted of a gold coin bra and belt. This set was so useful in both the folk styles and cabaret styles.

The most common belt type was called the "saddle belt." This consisted of a narrow base with a large half circle shape added to the back and a smaller half circle shape to the front. Keeping the front and back half circle shapes separate from the base made it easier for adjustment if weight was gained or lost. However, to save time, we often made the whole thing as one piece.

The most common bra type used was the push-up bra with a hard shell. The sides of the bra were cut away and two thin straps were added to the sides, giving it an open look. Today, the bra sides are fully covered and wide. This later change happened mainly due to the ease of construction and because the Egyptian costume, being like this, influenced our tastes.

We first covered our bra and belt with gold fabric like heavy lame or brocade. The standard beginning student's coin costume was partially covered in coin and partially in gold braid trim. This was often due to a tight budget. The upper portion of the bra cup and belt was the area we often trimmed in the gold braid. A few gold coins were hung from the loops of the braid trim. The coins on the lower half of the bra and belt were sewn with the fish-scale technique, which allowed the coin to overlap and cover the area properly.   Of course the coins would sound wonderful when shaken. Any empty areas on the top of the bra and belt were decorated with embroidery, shisha mirrors, or jewels depending on the effect you wanted. Finally we applied drapes of chain and coin to the bra and belt.

Photo A

Photo A: Photo courtesy of Middle Eastern Culture and Dance Association.   Model: Anaheed of Los Angeles (c.2012). Iconic go-to style for student or professional; this coin belt was made by Anaheed in the mid-1970's and has been refurbished several times over the years. Skirt and jacket made of green and gold Persian lace.

Professional gold coin costumes were sometimes fully covered with coin. These had rich belly drapes, full coin bras, and coin belts held together with heavy jump rings and set off with a special front piece.

Photo B: Model: Hadia of Canada (c.1978). Full coin set – head to toe. Hadia says she and her roommate Carol Boyce made the costume. Carol Boyce later had a costuming business named Hafi Harem. Hadia says she was taught that this was what "ethnic" belly dance costume was like, but later learned that Middle Eastern women never wore anything like this. Hadia's veil is a fine example of Assuit.

We used coins with two holes sewn flat to cover the whole belt, and then a second layer of coins would be hanging loosely to jingle against the first layer. We made our own coin percussion "playing our belts" along with the drum or in counter-point. In turn, our belly drapes bounced and shook to our stomach flutters. We added bells from India to enhance this effect.

Appliqués' were all the rage. We decorated cotton skirts , Persian lace skirts, Baladi dresses, and vests for the outdoor festival and the cabaret stage. Motifs of pyramids shapes were seen using Persian lace and middy braid designed by Samira-Costume-Maker. Samira, a California based vendor/dancer, traveled the USA selling her popular appliqué designs and was a national representative for The Lion in The Sun, a Persian Lace importer.

Photo C

Photo C: Photo courtesy of Herb Kissling. Model: Dawna Kissling of southern CA. Persian lace ensemble designed and made by Samira Costume-Maker in mid-70's. Jacket and over-skirt is all Persian lace decorated with silver middy braid, silver rickrack, and embroidered Jacquard trim. Bra & belt is beaded appliqué and seed bead fringe made by Dawna.
Photos: D&E: Close-up of Persian Lace appliqué detail.

Persian lace could be a subject on its own. The Lion In The Sun of California sold this imported metallic lace to an enthusiastic generation of dancers. Magnificent and colorful, most dancers of the day had at least one item made of it. According to the vendors I have spoken to, the fabric mills in Iran where it was made were destroyed when the Shah of Iran was deposed in 1979. There are only small amounts remaining here in the USA. The costumes made from this fabric are still in perfect condition today and are treasures in private collections.

Another fabric used prolifically was Assuit or "Tulle bi telle." The fabric Assuit was named after the city in which it was made. Strips of small flat silver pieces were woven and flattened into cotton or linen mesh, creating ornate and distinct patterns. We used the fabric in Baladi dresses, skirts, shawls, vests, and veils. This fabric is still available today, though more expensive and not as fine a weave in most cases.

Vests were popular and used in both outdoor festival performances and the nightclub scene. Today the term most used for vests is "choli," an Indian term. Back in the 70's, we called them Turkish or Arabic vest depending on the style and sometimes by the Turkish name "yelak" which means, "vest."

Turkish vests go under the bra leaving the bra fully visible. The Arabic style partially covered the lower half of the bra. Vests were used in folk and cabaret styles.

Layering was the theme of all costuming styles. This was due in part to the interest in Ethnic costume and also the huge influence of Jamila Salimpour's troupe Bal Anat. I can tell you that the more layers I put on, the more exotic I felt.

Photo F

Photo F: Photo courtesy of Sarah Munro (Samira). Model Aradia (Paula English) c.1978. Layers and more layers were Aradia's style and we all tried to emulate that look. Aradia had a way with blending prints and colors into a rich colorful costume. She was a unique dancer and designer.

In the 70's, everyone wore the Afghani dress. So comfortable because of the cotton and cotton-polyester blend fabrics, this dress was the go-to item to hang out in at festivals and even at home for fun. Authentic imported dresses were collected as treasures. The imported ones were covered with the embroidery patterns specific to whatever region it came from. The dresses were made of velvet, cotton, polyester, or silk or in combinations of these fabrics. Appliqué and beading were a part of the design.

Photo G

Photo G: Photo courtesy of Middle Eastern Culture and Dance Association. Model Tawni Tindell c.2012, This dress is part of Marguerite Garner's personal collection. It is an authentic Afghani dress from a mountain region of Afghanistan. This is a traditional wedding dress and is 40 to 50 years old.

The Folkwear pattern company made an Afghani dress pattern, which is still available today. Everyone I knew made at least one of these gorgeous comfortable dresses. The American version was beaded, covered in patchwork and trims, and often had a lower neckline. It was inspired by the authentic original, but distinctly different.

Photo H: Photo courtesy of Sarah Munro (Samira). Model Aradia (Paula English) c.1977. Here again is the talented Aradia showing off her unparalleled talent for mixing patterns in her version of the Afghani dress.

Stripes were a common theme among costume styles. In particular, striped skirts were admired and used in both the cabaret and outdoor festivals in America. They were often made of cotton blends, polyester fabrics, and silks. They were worn with coin or beaded bra and belt sets. To the beginning dancer, the skirt with stripes inspired visions of Bedouin tents and dancing on carpets.

Photo I: Model Jenza c.1978 at Coco's International Nightclub in Hollywood, CA. This gorgeous striped skirt is still in perfect condition today. It is polyester knit with red, silver, black and gold stripes.

Stripes, being extremely popular in Egypt, inspired American dancer-designers to copy the style in beaded flatwork on bras and belts using bugle beads and seed beads to create the look. Thin, red and silver, or black and gold stripes were very admired in the USA.

Photo J: Model Jenza c. 1983 at the Burger Continental in Pasadena, CA. This set was made mostly of bugle beads in the flatwork and the fringe along with some seed beads and beaded appliqué.

The most popular skirts were flowing full circles in the back and a half circle in the front in separate pieces in order to show off "lots of leg!" The 1970's was the decade of the layered skirts. Dancers most often wore two skirts. One or both skirts were pulled up on the side and stuffed artfully into our hip belts creating "poufs" of fabric. In the cabaret scene, lots of leg was the norm and these poufs framed a good set of legs with panache.

A carry-over style from the 50's/60's was the skirt with borders. This added extra excitement to a layered "look." They were made by cutting strips of fabric on the bias, folding the strips, and applying them to the bottom of the skirt. Fabrics used as borders were usually satin, brocade, or lame. Another popular technique was the overlay framed with trim. Overlay fabrics were most often sheer with embroidered patterns or metallic patterns. The weight of the skirt border created a beautiful flow as the dancer was spinning.

Skirt borders went out of fashion by the end of the 1970's. I personally believe this is partly due to the extra labor and cost involved.

Photo K: Model Jenza, c.1979 at the Apadana in Newport Beach, CA. This shows the typical layering of two skirts. Both skirts have borders created by the overlay method and framed in gold middy braid. The black underskirt is brought up to frame the opening at the legs and the grey/gold overskirt was brought up to stuff in behind the dark skirt. The overskirt was shear grey organza with tiny gold stripes running through it. The gold bra and belt is a mix of beads and coin. The belt is the typical skinny belt of the time period topped off with a beaded diamond front piece.

In the 60's, beaded bra and belt sets had a distinctive layered or 3-D look to them and looped fringe was common. As the 70's progressed flatwork beaded costuming became popular everywhere. We used bugle beads and seed beads to create patterns like the stripes I mentioned earlier. Fringe was more often hanging straight and often layered in levels, and by the mid-1980's long monster fringe was all the rage.

Belt shapes became thinner on the sides and back with common centerpieces being diamonds and half circles. The centerpieces were separate and could be removed to adjust for weight fluctuations. Flatwork took months to do. This is likely the reason for the thinner bases of the belts. Skinnier belts equal less time involved.

The most glorious cabaret costume piece of the 70's was the cape! Usually made of transparent organza, it flowed magnificently and made a dancer feel like a queen. Capes were often constructed with layers of ruffles giving it a fluffier look. The cape created a truly dramatic entrance and was best used on a large stage. Great care had to be taken to avoid catching your cape on the musician's instruments if the stage was small.

Capes were sewn together just like a sleeveless coat with openings for the arms to go through.

The front of the cape was often tucked in on the bra straps to keep it from slipping and for quick removal later in the show. Loops were sewn to the bottom, and then attached to our little fingers. Finger cymb-als were played with ease while the cape was looped around the little finger. The cape would swirl magnificently.

Photo M: Photo courtesy of Ilia Wilkin. Model Samrah Masoud c.1978. This luscious cape was made by famous dancer/designer Nadia Simone. This particular cape shows off rows and rows of ruffles and really flows well due to the lightness of the organza. This picture was taken at the first fundraiser of the Middle Eastern Cabaret Dancer's Association for which Samrah was president and founder.

I would like to thank Mezdulene for the opportunity to share my passion about 1970's belly dance costuming with her Jareeda readers! Dance on.

About the author:

Jenza (Suzanne McNeil) is a 2nd generation dancer of a 3-generation Belly Dance family in the Los Angeles area, consisting of her mother Samira (Sarah Munro) and her daughter Elayssa Thomson. Jenza is the creator of the Historical Belly Dance Fashion Show and recently The Story of Belly Dance in America-1893 to 1979, a dance show depicting the history and foundations of Belly Dance in America. See **www.jenza.com**.

KHALEEGY

By Halima

Khaleegy pronounced "kuh-lee-jee" is the Arabic word for gulf. You will sometimes see it spelled as Khaleeji and Khaliji. It is also called Saudi, Gulf Dance, Hair Dance and Women's Dance. It is also called Raks na'ashar to distinguish it from some of the men's dance and in Kuwait it is called Samra or Samri. It is a folk dance from the Persian Gulf, i.e., Saudi Arabia, Kuwait, Bahrain, Qatar, United Arab Emirates and Oman. The rhythm is simply called Khaleegy or Saudi.

The Khaleegy dress or Thobe Al Nasha'ar is a beautiful extra long dress that is usually a solid color fabric with delicate embroidery of gold and silver and/or pearls on the front and along the sleeves. The back is usually plain. The sleeves are very open and long; this allows the person to

pull the sleeve onto their head and use it as a face veil. These beautiful thobes can be worn over anything but I remember being told that the dress that was worn beneath them was called a Fustan which was simply a shift type dress. Some of the Thobes that I see now actually look more like caftans with a more fitted sleeve. These would be a little hard to perform the exact same style of dance as the longer ones with the larger sleeves.

Photos are Mas'uda Dance Troupe

This dance is usually performed at weddings and social gatherings. The Thobe is never worn to parties but simply taken there and changed into upon arrival. The dance is usually performed in pairs or two lines with the women passing each other. The women will ululate and talk to each other when passing, giving encouragement. Sometimes the women will take turns leading the dance with the others following. This does give a lot of creativity for floor patterns if you are performing this dance in a show.

The hair which is worn loose is swung in a circular, figure eight motion, or a pulsing motion where the head is dropped twice to each side flinging the hair as you change from one side to the other. I heard someone once remark that the flinging the hair to one side and pulsating reminded them of trying to get water out of their ears. Hopefully that will give you a more visual aspect of the movement. While performing the hair movements one or both hands are placed palm down on the chest. I have also seen the hair movements performed with one hand placed along the side of the nose as though you were whispering something.

The basic footwork is simple using a limping type step with one foot flat and the other on the ball, i.e., flat, ball, flat (Right, Left, Right) or simply a two step flat, ball (R,L). The movements come mostly from the shoulders, hips, and hair and hand gestures. The hands pick up the thobe and make circular and figure eight movements. There is also a hand movement where the hands pull the thobe to one side and the hands are close together and move up and down opposite of each other in a vertical movement, i.e., right, left right, and then left, right, left to the music. When the emphasis is on the hands, the motions are smaller and more delicate. Hand flutters are common with usually one hand holding the thobe while the other makes the fluttering motion. When the emphasis is on the thobe the motions are quite large, i.e., swinging the thobe in a figure eight motion, pulling it to one side while turning or doing hip movements so that the hip motion can be seen. You are showing off your beautiful thobe so that everyone can admire it.
The shoulder motions are small rocking movements with the emphasis on shoulders rather than the bust. Also head slides and head circles are used in this dance as well.

thelightcatcher@gmail.com

Hand gestures in the Middle East usually have some meaning. For example, an Egyptian hand gesture called Al Assal is when the dancer places her fingertips to side of the chin; this gesture indicates "sweet as honey." Fingers to forehead mean "happiness." So always try to identify hand gestures before using them if possible. Another hand movement I have seen is where the hands are palm to palm resembling that of a fish and what I call "Allah" hands where the hands are uplifted as though in supplication.

When performed properly this is one of the most beautiful feminine dances I have ever seen. It is shy, coy, flirtatious, never vulgar and always joyful. Remember the emphasis in this dance is on delicate, graceful movements.

Dance and be joyful!

About the author

Halima has been involved in Middle Eastern Dance since 1976. I have studied, taught and performed both cabaret and folkloric styles throughout the United States. I have been a member of the Sahda Dance Co, Baklava Dance Ensemble and the artistic director for Sisters of the Sun, The Nile Dancers and Chandi Dance Co.

I have served as an officer and editor of MEDECA Magazine for over six years. I'm also a former editor of Jareeda Magazine.

I'm a costume designer and have owned Halima's Designs for 35 years. My love for Middle Eastern Dance is reflected in the time and hard work I put into promoting this dance form. I love sharing the knowledge an continually try to acquire more. I find the sharing process the most rewarding on a personal level.

I was the originator and president of Midnight Oasis Production Co. and have been instrumental in bringing many well-known artists to the Pacific Northwest. I was also one of the originators of La Danse Orientale Belly Dance Competition in Oregon and have revived it in Washington with my friend and partner, Gilana. I was also one of the originators of the Belly Dancer Showcase which is now hosted by Saqra as Saqra's Showcase. I have judged many competitions and was instrumental in writing much of the current contest judging criteria for several competitions.

I have been interviewed by several publications and on the cover of the 1989 December issue of Caravan Magazine. I'm also the recipient of the MEDECA award for outstanding long term support of MEDECA and Middle Eastern Damce, the recipient of the 1990 Magana Babtiste Achievement award, two time winner of the Nafisa award for promotion of the dance and the Double Crown lifetime achievement award, the 2004 recipient of the Mystical Oasis lifetime achievement award and the Emerald Rain competition sisterhood award.

I'm proud of my accomplishments simply because it demonstrates my love and devotion to this dance form that has stolen my heart. I continue to study as much as I can feeling that we are all eternal students.
Photo is Halima in 1982

THEATRICAL EVENTS and the (RE)CONSTRUCTION of CULTURAL MEMORIES

by "Morocco" (Carolina Varga Dinicu) ©2002 & 20014

For the **Kel Tagelmousse**, the Blue People of the Tuareg of the Sahara Desert (which stretches from Mauritania to the border of Egypt), **Guedra** is a trance ritual of blessing not only of great importance to them, but one which commanded such respect in Morocco that King Hassan II had his own official **Guedra**, a woman named **B'Shara**, who did it to bless many important events. Unfortunately, except for extremely watered - down snippets for tourist dinner shows, it has almost disappeared in its original, ritualistic form due to several factors, especially the 40+ year drought in the Sahara and the resulting necessity for too many Blue People to move into cities in order to survive (leading to several of their long-held traditions and rituals being lost/ended); an understandable desire to assimilate into the prevailing City culture in which they now found themselves (far more patriarchal than their own in the desert); and the desire to be – or at least appear "up-to- date"/ modern.

At a private event in 1963 in New York City, I first saw a bit of real **Guedra**, thanks to an amazing stroke of luck, done by three women from **B'shara**'s group, who would also be doing it at the Moroccan Pavillion for the 1964 World's Fair in Flushing Meadow Park in Queens. What they did and its effects on me were so mesmerizing, I wanted more. To satisfy my own personal curiosity and thirst for knowledge, I borrowed the plane fare from my mother, flew to Casablanca and set off by train, bus, jeep and donkey-back for Goulmime, Morocco (on the edge of the Sahara) later that year. What we, in the West, prefer to call "luck" connected me with the aforementioned **B'Shara**, who, during the time I was there and on subsequent visits, taught me all she could about the ritual and the life/ culture of the Blue People, because the two are inseparable.

Unlike *Zar* (from Sudan, but also popular in Egypt's poorer sections), *Hadra* (from Morocco) and Tunisia's *Stambouli*, also trance rituals, but whose purpose is to appease or exorcise "demons," thereby often curing minor psychosomatic and real illnesses, also, incidentally, the only real "socially acceptable" outlets for female frustration in areas where their public behavior is very circumscribed and must be at all times beyond reproach, the **Guedra** is a *blessing* ritual, wherein the intent is to "channel" all the "good forces" and feelings of peace and soul's love from the center of the earth, sending them out into the world via the fingertips of the female **Guedra** or "vessel," blessing all those present in person or in spirit with "good energy" - spiritual love, not carnal - transmitted from the depths of the guedra's soul via her fingers and hands. A female, not an intermediary spirit (**djinn** or **afrit**) delivers the message/ the "force." **Only** a female can be a **Guedra.**

Some necessary backround/explanation: in a nomadic society, such as the Blue People's, what can be carried by one person or animal is limited, so every item must be essential and multi-purpose. In **Darija (**Moroccan Arabic), the word "**guedra**" means cauldron/ cooking pot/ vessel.

That vessel could be covered with an animal skin to make a drum, also called "*guedra*", to play the heart-beat rhythm (life's basic rhythm) – also called "*guedra*", for the female performer, the "vessel," also called a "*Guedra,*" of the actual ritual, which is also called "*Guedra*" - *but* only as long as it is being done on the knees. When the "*Guedra*" doing it stands up (or starts the ritual standing up), it is called *T'bal*. In the 50 years I've been researching, doing and teaching *Guedra*, nobody from there has been able to explain the reason for the difference in the names - not even my teacher, B'shara. However, I have come to my own conclusions, based on language and imagery, which I won't go into here.

The Blue People's society is egalitarian: unusual enough in terms of "Western" cultures (who presume to call it "matriarchal" because the women have equality and respect in some areas considered "male" here), but almost unbelievable in context of what is mistakenly assumed to be "Islamic"..

Guedra isn't a dance, it is a ritual, one in which anybody and everybody can participate, although the central figure/s is/ are the female *Guedra/s* (sometimes two women do it together, or a man and woman or woman and child of either sex). The accompaniment consists of the drum (*guedra*), which can also be played by anyone, of any sex or age, with the skill and desire to do so, and rhythmical clapping and chanting by any and all others present. Nowadays, a gourd instrument that is slapped and shaken is sometimes added. Chants are in *Tamahaq* (their language) or *Darija* (Moroccan Arabic) and can be about anything, from religious to praise or comments about the king or expressions of thanks for good fortune or a wish granted. Most often, they call upon God and goodness, to be shared with all humanity.

Clothing often has a tremendous effect on movements of dances and rituals, especially in those ethnic forms, where tradition leaves very little leeway for individual choice or expression. Those garments, their styles and reasons for being that way, usually pre-date dances and rituals done while wearing them. Not so theater dance, where costumes are (hopefully) designed to facilitate and accentuate the choreography, though exceptions do exist, or to portray a specific historical period or class, a character, an idea or symbol.

The Blue woman's unique headdress is also a result of adaptation to desert conditions - and germane to the overall effect of the *Guedra*. Anywhere from two to six inches high (or more), the front is made of leather, canvas, felt or woven horsehair decorated with cowry shells, silver coins, turquoise, coral and the occasional mother-of-pearl button or Coca-Cola bottle top. From this front, a circlet of wire, bent twigs or bone sits on the crown of the head and the wearer's hair, interwoven with horsehair and braided over and down, fastens it firmly to the head. Cowrie shells, silver, turquoise and coral beads are also woven into the multiple braids. From the back of the circlet, a "handle" rises to the same height as the front piece, up and over the center of the head, approaching but not touching the front "crown." Horsehair or wool is woven around it. Such a time-consuming and elaborate hairdo is usually redone every one and a half to two months. The headdress supports the aforementioned two-meter fabric end/ veil, keeping it off the the wearer's head and leaving an air space that maintains her normal body temperature of 98.6F, thereby keeping her cooler in the heat of the day and warmer in the cold desert night.

Guedra is a nighttime ritual, around a fire under the light of the moon or inside one of the larger tents. When done for real, as versus for an audience, it's most often in a circle. The drum throbs with the heartbeat rhythm and the clapping starts. Shrill *zagareet* (ululations) ring out, the chanting swells. Inspiration calls, a woman from the circle answers: for now, she is the *Guedra*. Pulling the tail of her robe over her headdress, so it covers her head, face and chest, she puts on the "magic" necklace. It's up to her as to whether she starts standing up or on her knees.

The "veil" covering the *Guedra*'s head, shoulders and chest signifies darkness, the unknown, lack of knowledge. Her hands and fingers are moving under the covering, flicking at it, trying to escape into the light. When she feels the time is right, the her hands emerge, one at a time, from the veil's sides. With hand-to-head gestures, she salutes the four corners: North, South, East and West, followed by obeisances to the four elements: Fire (the sun), Earth, Wind and Water. She touches her abdomen, heart and head, then quickly flicks her fingers towards all others present, in life or spirit, sending blessings to them from the depths of her soul's energy, as if she were sending little bursts of lightning or holy water …..

In the *Guedra*, the vast majority of movement flows from the fingers and hands, with some arm movement from the elbows down. The ribcage is lifted and lowered, as in many African dances. When extra emphasis is called for the head can be gently turned from side-to-side, causing the braids to sway. As the *Guedra* comes to a crescendo, accent in the chest movements transfers from lift to lowering and the head swings more strongly from side-to-side with chin lifts, causing her braids to "fly." When done "for real", a *Guedra* goes on for quite a time, gradually increasing in tempo and intensity, but still keeping the heartbeat rhythm. Likewise, the *Guedra's* breathing also increases in depth and intensity, until she collapses in a trance.

When a man joins in, it is as an accompaniment, to induce a woman of his choice to accept the magic necklace from him and bless him - and the others with her soul's energy via the *Guedra*. After she accepts and takes the necklace, he unfolds the shoulder drapings of his *dra*, holding it out in his fingers to its full width, dipping and swaying from side to side, until she is ready to focus her energy and go on with the ritual alone. In the group, the men concentrate on driving and maintaining the clapping and chanting that encourage the *Guedra* and deepen her trance. Blue people consider *Guedra* their direct contact with the elements, spirits and universe, the deepest expression of their souls and protection against a hostile environment and evil spirits.

Getting a usable soundtrack was virtually impossible for a lone researcher, given the year I first went (1963) and circumstances: real *Guedra* is performed at night, in the open desert, around a fire – ergo no electricity, no battery operated iPods or iPads with good sound quality even existed back then, lots of sand everywhere, getting into everything, not to mention peripheral conversations, diversions, etc. among those present. Add to that my observations over many years of research in myriad cirumstances and almost every condition possible, that the minute any *visible* recording device appears, the dynamic immediately changes and becomes something other than "spontaneous" or "authentic" – *not* what I went there to get.

In 1976 my amazing "luck" again came into play: Rachid el Idrissi, one of the two men responsible for the Moroccan Pavillion and that gala at which I first saw *Guedra*, arranged for a special evening of *Guedra and Schikhatt* on the grounds of King Hassan II's Marrakesh palace, just for me and the tour group I'd organized to see the Marrakesh Folk Festival. It was still outdoors, still at night around a fire, **but** there was a nearby windowsill, an extension cord and a tiny cassette recorder, invisible to those doing the ritual. *Only* drawback: the loudest frogs I've ever heard come through at the beginning of the tape, then they mysteriously shut up. I now had about an hour of various chants, usable in different sequences and circumstances.

What made me think such an intense interactional ritual could even work on a stage? The first time I saw just a bit of it, incongruously presented in the midst of that gala dinner for an **haute couture** fashion show, it totally transfixed me and the rest of that jaded crowd. I could only imagine what a fuller theater presentation might do. To share with a non-"native" theater/ dance public what I found so mesmerizing about this and other wonderful but rapidly disappearing ethnic dances of the Middle East and North Africa that I had learned "in culture" - which were mostly group endeavors as versus solos - I decided to form a dance company, a daunting enough task in any circumstances, but much more so in a country where Arts and artists – especially in non-mainstream ethnic dance - are left to flounder alone, unsupported financially, but also mostly unrestricted. Thus the Casbah Dance Experience was born in 1977.

Choreographing/ implementing how to best present **Guedra** in a theater/ performance setting, being true to it without seriously compromising it, presented quite a unique challenge because this was not a dance, able to charm with its grace, musicality and movement technique, but a ritual of mostly specific and proscribed hand and finger movements, one that was usually done outdoors, under the night sky, in an intimate circle around a fire.... Most of the performances my new dance company would be doing were also outdoors, but during the day, in sunlight, in parks and on open-air stages or in church and youth center gymnasiums and dance rooms, under fluorescent lights, where the audience was at a distance. There was no large budget for scenery or props, no vehicles to get us and our things there and back: transportation was courtesy of the New York subway system. Prop, music and costume transport - what we could carry in our own hands.

Were the movements difficult for my dancers to master? The problems – and larger ones than might be assumed - were that the movements are seemingly **so** simple, the real difficulties lay in preventing them from trying to embellish or make the movements more "Oriental"/ graceful and in making the specific, limited movement vocabulary of this ritual varied and interesting enough in its presentation that the audience "gets it." Specific flicks of specific fingers, a bit of hand and arm movement, some rising and falling of the ribcage/ chest, their sequence and repetition, minimal movement of feet or "travelling." Who does what, when and with whom. Why? What should I add to or subtract from the presentation make it work? An actual **Guedra** could last hours...

I shortened it considerably, then opened the circle into a semi-circle, letting the audience in, as it were. After false starts with chant sequences that felt either too long or short, thereby probably resulting in either boredom or seeming chaos, I found four different chants that seemed to work together, splicing them into a 10 ½ minute sequence. I devised a "story" with "characters," for audience involvement and understanding, starting with some dancers already seated, as if waiting for the rest to arrive. The others come, already veiled by the tail end of their *haiks*, each greeting the two main **Guedras**, who are seated back center of the semi-circle on either side of the lone male (only had one male dancer in my company at the time!), one at a time, with the triple clasped hand-to-head salute of the Blue People. They seat themselves at either end of the semi-circle and join in the rhythmical clapping and swaying.

One dancer from each end rises to a kneeling position, they slowly approach and pass each other stage front, blessing the stage area and dancers. As they cross in the center, another *Guedra* rises and starts towards center downstage, doing *T'bal* and blessing those in the audience and semi-circle. The first two perform some of the ritual's movements at the opposite ends of the semi-circle, then re-cross, sit in their original places, uncover their heads and join the clapping. The first chant is over, blending into the second one.

The two main *Guedras*, representing a bride and her mother, cover their heads and shoulders with the tail ends of their *haiks*, rise from their seated positions and do the next chant standing (*T'bal*), crossing from side to side, one behind the other, circling back to back, facing each other, then the others on stage then the audience, together then apart. The second chant ends, and a third, more intense one starts. They uncover their faces, blessing all present, make several turns and sink to their knees to really "get into" the *Guedra*. As the third chant ends, the "mother," still on her knees, returns to her place in the circle, sits and the male stands, holding his dagger by its corded belt.

We are about to incorporate the *Betrothal Dance of Tissint* into this *Guedra* Suite. He approaches the still kneeling "bride," who rises and starts fluttering her shoulders like a frightened bird, moving away from the "groom," who pursues her in a circle, his proferred dagger the offering of his protection - an official "proposal"! After a bit of his pursuing her all around the semi-circle and stage front, she turns to face him, approaches and stops long enough to allow him to slip the dagger's belt over her head, signifying her acceptance of his proposal. If this were Tissint, they would now be betrothed.

She again drops to her knees and finishes the *Guedra*, simulating going into a trance. The fourth chant ends with the groom encircling/ covering the tranced-out young *Guedra* with the long, flowing sleeves of his *ghandura* or *'dra*. Curtain or lights out.

Why did I combine *Guedra* with the *Betrothal Dance*? The women's clothing and movements aren't the same for both, but the man's clothing and his manner of holding the magic/ blessed necklace out to the *Guedra* of his choice were almost exactly the same. I wanted a bit of "drama", wanted a real role for the male dancer and I had an artistic license, so I exercised it.

Did my dancers find the rehearsals and the "tableau" boring or repetitious? Did I get attitude? Not from the ones who had been to Morocco or were of African-American heritage: they understood totally and produced some very effective and affecting performances. Once I explained what it was about, the rest did too and really got into it, even in rehearsals. How were rehearsals different from normal? I gave my dancers more leeway to develop their characters and movements – within the context of the authentic vocabulary – than I ordinarily would have, rather than teach them a set choreography, thus making it easier for them to find the emotion and its expressions and get them across to the audience.

Was it difficult to find or make the costumes and headpieces? I live in New York City, home of the garment district and wholesale fabric stores, have a sewing machine, dancers who also did and could sew. I brought back several authentic fibulae and a few tourist copies that were more than good enough for the stage and a real headdress that we could then copy – though it was very time-consuming. Dark blue and black cotton was easy to get, so it was not difficult to design something a dancer could get into easily and quickly, looked as real as the actual thing, which was more complex and would have required far more time to get into or out of – especially the headdress. In this way, we could do the *Guedra* as the opening tableau, put a soloist or two on afterwards and change for the next group dance.

Did my experience with other rituals (Dervish, *Zar*, *Hadra*...) help or inform my interpretation of *Guedra*? Of course! Being aware that there were many rituals still existing in these areas, each unique, really helped me not to fall into the trap of assuming what went for one, went for the other. I strove assiduously as I could to respect and honor what it was that made *Guedra* so effective and affecting.

A student, now a member of the Casbah Dance Experience asked me: "What did you keep for authenticity's sake that you weren't sure would work in the presentation?" I kept everything, except a real fire on stage, the "blessed/ magic necklace" or actually going into trance. No fire or actual trance for obvious reasons. Where the necklace was concerned, it took too much time to take off, drape the covering over the headdress and put back on, fine when the *Guedra* had lots of time, but really breaking the "spell" within such a short context.

What was I unsure of?? Everything. Nothing like this had ever been seen in this form in America, certainly not within the context of the slowly burgeoning Oriental dance scene, still very suspect in theater circles (the man who hired us for that performance was putting his job on the line to do so!) and I was risking my entire reputation when I debuted it and my dance company at Lincoln Center in August 1978. However, the more I learned about and did *Guedra*, the more certain I was that I had to take that chance and go for it.

Lincoln Center's Damrosch theater is outdoors, but has good lighting and sound and a very cooperative backstage crew. It was a warm summer night. Too anxious back then to trust *Guedra* as the opening number, it started the second half, in half-light, gradually working it up to full after the "greetings" as the two kneeling *Guedras* started across the floor. Ten and a half minutes can seem like years. When the tape ended, there was total silence. "Omigod, I thought: we're dead in the water! They didn't like it." Three seconds passed, then waves of applause broke out and shouts of "Bravo!" I could now exhale!

The rest of the concert went very well and when it was over, many waited at the stage door, to ask about the *Guedra*, saying that they could feel the waves of love and blessing washing over them, as the dancers' fingers flicked it at them. This *without* any detailed explanation in the program, which simply listed the names of the dances and the dancers. We now open all our concerts with a *Guedra*, either the group tableau or me doing it as a solo. Over the years, the response has been overwhelmingly positive and many, many audience members have come, sometimes with tears in their eyes, to tell me that they "got" it and felt really blessed. I must admit, so do I.

I was asked if I ever did *Guedra* as a solo before staging it with the troupe – not for an audience, but with my teacher, B'shara and her Blue People: I learned by assimilating and doing. Then, when I was asked to teach it at dance seminars all over the United States and Europe, it was impossible to take the whole troupe, so I started doing it solo, all 10 ½ minutes, but with a longer entrance/ salutation, coming on to the stage through the audience, and no "Betrothal Dance", but full-out *Guedra* till the end.

How do the Blue People feel about non-Moroccan dancers performing their ritual as performance? I asked them, years ago. They were shocked at first, then thrilled that anybody outside of their country even knows it exists, let alone cares enough to learn it properly and perform it in theaters and with respect. In their own country, they've seen it bowdlerized, condensed, thrown at tourists' in careless, minute-long snippets at "cultural" evening Fantasias and dinner tent shows.

It has been suggested to me that the reconstructed, performed *Guedra* perhaps creates a new kind of memory -- with what I sincerely hope is much, much more than a trace of the original, a sense for audiences that they are experiencing a "real" cultural practice. Does something of the ritual's function survive in its theatrical form? YES! And I have been unbelievably fortunate to have had the unique opportunity to introduce it in this manner to thousands of people, who would never have had the opportunity to experience it in any other way. Many, also intrigued by what I was able to show them in one performance or seminar/ explanation situation, have come to me to learn more and gone on to perform and teach it themselves.

It took the Beatles, Rolling Stones, Joe Cocker and other "foreigners" to bring real American music, that had long been unappreciated and underestimated at home because of its origins in Black music, back to the USA. To me, *Guedra* represents an important cultural memory, transformed by an "outsider" into a performance situation that just might be truer to its origins than one finds in its present-day but modernized "back yard", with aesthetic conventions that could possibly be the true link to preserve the actual ritual for loving return to its original "owners" - an example of how reality made into theater rescues the continuity of that reality.

About the Author

Morocco (Carolina Varga Dinicu) is considered the leading performer and authority in her field in the U.S., Canada and abroad, evidenced by frequent invitations to teach master seminars and perform in Germany, Sweden, Norway, Austria, Switzerland, Finland, Holland, Luxembourg, Australia, Israel, Malaysia, Brazil, the UK, Slovenia, the Czech Republic, Panama, Italy, Greece, Morocco, Turkey, China and Egypt.

She is the author of "You Asked Aunt Rocky: Answers & Advice About Raqs Sharqi & Raks Shaabi," a book that includes over fifty years of research and experience! It has received numerous 5-star reviews and is fast becoming the go-to-book in the field. It has been translated into Chinese and German.

Since 1964, Morocco has written for several publications in her field and been reprinted in dance, medical and feminist publications internationally. A true pioneer in the field, she taught a 3-credit course in Middle Eastern Dance and Culture at the State University of New York in the mid 1970s.

She continues her extensive performing career as a soloist and created the Casbah Dance Experience to show the varied, fascinating ethnic dances of the Middle East and North Africa to the general public and give "a bit of home" to North Africans and Mideasterners in the West. She's spent over 53 years trying to find, recover, preserve and present them before they disappear, due to modernization and/or fundamentalism. It's a valuable heritage that must be saved from extinction!

Morocco collects all music, steps and styles possible of each dance from many on-site viewings, questions and participation and chooses a variety of the most typical steps and figures, presenting them in choreography true to their origins, while pleasing to the eyes and ears of the theater public.

Morocco led many highly successful dance/culture tours to Morocco, Egypt and Turkey, introducing Western performers, teachers and fans of these dances to the rich variety of music and dance indigenous to those areas. She's taught at SUNY-Purchase and Amas Repertory Theater and continues to teach at her own Academy of Mideastern Dance in NYC.

Morocco opened the door for Mideastern Oriental dance in museums, schools, at Lincoln Center, SUNY-Purchase and as a valid, valuable concert form. Research has taken her to Morocco, Egypt, Tunisia, Algeria, Lebanon, Syria, Jordan, Iraq, Iran, Turkey, Azerbaijan, Uzbekistan, Turkmenistan, Kazakhstan, Tadjikistan, Kirghizia, Georgia, Armenia, Greece, Yugoslavia, etc.

Morocco continues to teach, research, write, lecture and perform and hopes to keep on *"till 6 weeks after I'm dead"*……

Photo by Miss Katherine Lawrence of Liverpool, UK

THE SOUL OF BELLY DANCE TOUCHES MY OWN SOUL

By Mezdulene Bliss

The soul is not something you can see; it's not something you can measure. The soul is a person's essence, their spirit, that miraculous and mysterious thing that makes them unique and distinctive in a world of over seven billion other souls.

Many people of many different faiths from around the world believe in reincarnation. The belief is that after death, the soul is released from the body, exists in a pure spiritual state and then returns via a new body, and that it learns from each incarnation and eternally progresses to higher planes of spiritual awareness and bliss. There is also the belief that there are young souls and old souls.

So, in my mind I see the soul traveling through time from inception to the present and taking lessons from each life it experiences, and this is much the same way I see belly dance.

Belly dance, Raks Sharqi, Le Danse Orientale, Middle Eastern dance; call it what you will, it has a life of its own and has gone from the Middle East to around the globe from before written history to the space age, and all along the way it has gained something new and different with each person it has come in contact with.

In ballet, first position is first position whether it's done in America or anywhere. Swan Lake choreography is the same all over the world. My dance has no such standards and no limitations. Each dancer is free to interpret the music in their own way, to create without limitations and allow their own essence to shine.

And speaking of music, what would the dance be without it? The music has also evolved over centuries of musicians expressing it in their own way, each adding their own unique essence.

I see some belly dancers only comfortable with choreography, feeling that by choreographing each movement they are expressing each note of the music more completely.

For me, choreography leaves out the soul. Don't get me wrong. I use choreography for my troupe and dancing with my troupe is fun like going to Disneyland fun. But feeling the dance on a soul level is impossible for me while my brain is engaged to remember what step comes next.

As a soloist, I allow the music to come into me and to become a part of me, a part of who I am in that moment. Sometimes a piece of music will touch me so deeply that I dance to it repeatedly, but each time I dance it's a different dance. Every time I dance to a piece of music, even if it's twice in the same day, I'm a different person. I might be in a different mood, different location, different costume, just had a deep conversation or an angry one, so how could I possibly express the music in the same way?

I once saw a video of a top name dancer doing a choreographed routine. The video showed her dancing in different costumes throughout the same dance. In other words, she did the dance in six different costumes and then it was edited together. Her choreography was flawless, and she obviously danced it exactly the same in each costume, but there was no 'feeling' to her dance. I thought maybe it just didn't come across in the video and went to see her in person. There was still no feeling, flawless technique, but no feeling. It was like watching a robot dancing.

I've seen the same thing in musicians, perfect technique but no emotion, no depth, no soul.

For me, this dance is all about feeling, and allowing the music to tap into my core and then expressing that passion in the moment as it's happening, being my authentic self in each moment.

And that's how I remember dancers. I remember the ones who share their essence as they dance and forget the technicians.

I'm not making any judgments, just sharing what the dance means to me. The robot dancer? She's making the big bucks, so she's obviously doing something right. And that's what makes our art form so very powerful. It can be technical or mystical and everything in between appealing to a huge range of women.

My left-brained dance sisters bemoan the lack of structure while we right-brained dancers relish the lack of structure because a lack of structure means a lack of limitations. It's all perfect and what makes our dance such a fascinating and complex method of expression.

The belly dance that I do is an amalgamation of many countries throughout the Middle East. I do Arabic basics, Egyptian walks, Persian cross points, Tunisian twists, Moroccan toe pounds and so many many more.

While I know these names were mostly made up by Americans trying to create some kind of standard of communication, I imagine each one to have a bit of the essence of the country it's named after.

And, speaking of American; we added the beautiful art of veil dancing to an already incredible art form. The added spectacle of beautiful fabric gracefully flowing through the air is, in my opinion, a wonderful addition to the art of our dance.

I can't explain how I felt when I first started learning to belly dance other than to say it was like coming home, like I felt a connection on a deep level that I can only explain as something ancient. I had never seen belly dancing and knew nothing about it, but at my first class when my teacher did a demonstration dance, I was captivated, entranced and hooked for life. It was like a missing part of me or what Shamans call a soul part, came back to me and it was a wonderful feeling.

As I share the dance with other women, we become connected on an inner level. Women from all walks of life who had absolutely nothing in common before they came to class become fast friends as they become part of the dance community. Dance events become like family reunions as dancers greet and hug each other, as they take classes and perform together and as they share technique and costuming tips and stories.

And as dancers gather, they learn from each other either directly through classes, or by watching each other and becoming inspired with new movements and ideas.

While some dancers think there is a correct way to dance, I say there is no right and wrong. And, while some dancers think their way is the only true Middle Eastern dance or that Egyptian classic is the purest form of dance and lots of other bunk, it's obvious to me that our dance is a true art form. And like all art, it has evolved over time and continues to evolve.

There is no right or wrong; there is only the dance. And, as we each add the spice of ourselves to the mix, it becomes even more compelling and filled with soul.

When I visited Egypt many years ago, I performed in several night clubs, and while I was captivated by the Egyptian dancers, what surprised me was that they were equally captivated by me. While I wanted to learn from them, they also wanted to learn from me. And even though I didn't speak Arabic, and they didn't speak a word of English, we communicated with sign language and facial expressions and the occasional interpreter. This is the soul of belly dance, that sacred something that reaches across cultural boundaries, crosses borders and creates bridges between people of all races and belief systems. That power of art that touches us on a deep and profound level making us want to become even more intimate with it and more driven to experience it as much as possible.

This is a woman's dance. Yes, men belly dance also, but it's a feminine art form that has been passed down through generation after generation of women from mother to child and will continue to be passed down to generations to come.

As a teacher of belly dance, a part of me will live on through my students, and my student's students, another aspect of the soul of belly dance. As it has touched me, a spark of myself has touched and added something to it. And as my students become teachers, they add their own special essence. The Native Americans believe that what we do now impacts the seventh generation. I believe that when I teach belly dance, it goes even further, that the dance I do has spanned centuries and will continue on for many more centuries.

If you watch old films, you can see what the dance looked like 50 or more years ago, and today it looks quite different. I can't begin to imagine what it will morph into in the future.

Belly dance is a dance that makes women feel comfortable in their own skin, elevates them emotionally and connects them spiritually. It's transforming as well as fun, and there is nothing else like it. It's not limited to just the athletic or svelte, it speaks to all women regardless of age or size. It alters lives and creates healing from wounds thought to be untouchable.

There is a power to belly dance that goes beyond the physical realm, and its soul touches my soul.   Who knew?

About the Author

Mezdulene is passionate about Middle Eastern Dance, and she has been performing and teaching for over 30 years. She has taken classes and seminars with dozens of nationally and internationally known instructors and performed hundreds of times in concerts, night clubs, nursing homes, festivals and benefits. She has won many competitions in the professional, troupe and specialty categories.

Mezdulene is a master teacher and teaches from the heart and soul. She goes beyond technique to the core of the dance, helping students express their own individual essence. She believes that belly dance is the most creative and expressive dance form, giving us a unique and feminine outlet for personal expression. She loves watching her students blossom, gaining not only a new skill but also self-confidence, poise and pride in their own femininity.

The Art of Andre

Editor's Note: I thought it would be fun to end this book with a photographic journey through time with Andre Ebling, master photographer of belly dancers all over the world, as he shares 25 years of photos.

André Elbing born 1965 in Germany - Cologne, became interested in Oriental dance in 1989 when he started organizing and producing shows with his long time friend, Shahrazad. As he began taking photographs at some of the shows his business grew into an extensive collection of photographs of oriental dancers - about 2.000.000 photos in all.

Mr. Elbing has devoted the last 25 years of his career to oriental dance photography and has worked with the great stars of the oriental dance world, past and present. He has been published in several oriental dance magazines including Halima (D), Orient Magazine (D), Tanz Oriental (D), Bazar Oriental (D), Bastet (D), Chorika (D), Arabeske (D), Arabesque (USA), Karawane,(D) Caravan (USA), Tantra (D), Spirit (D), Habibbi (USA), EL GAWHARA (Egypt), Al Maqam (D), Jareeda (USA), Zaghareet (USA), Bennu (USA), Rakas (Australia), Elraks (Egypt), Elsharki(Egypt), Passion Orientale (F), Belly Divas, Al Ahram,(Egypt) Bellydance Magazine (USA), Wendy (NL), Layalina (Egypt), Danza Pyramids (E) …..you find his Photos on hundreds of Bellydance Internet pages and also on CD & DVD Covers, Books and so on. His book "Aesthetics and Mysticism - Danse Oriental" will be available in the spring of 2015. He specializes in photographing live performances, yet he has the ability to bring the harmony and magic of the performance into a studio photo session. He captures the moment in a way that draws the viewer in, making one feel a part of the performance. His landscape and portrait photography captivate the viewer as well. Exhibitions in Albuquerque, New York, Los Angeles, San Francisco, Katmandu, Berlin, Rostock, Cologne, Düsseldorf, Saarbrücken, Frankfurt, etc. are proof of the international interest in this art.

Furthermore he does decorations and moderations for Oriental Events and Shows from 10 up to 1001 guests and artists and organizes grandiose festivals.

André is a sincere philanthropist of Oriental Dance. Trips to the Orient, Europe, Russia and to the United States enabled him to bring artists of the "Danse Oriental" together for new projects and thus promote this unique art form.

1989 Rose

1993 Zarefah

1996 Dina

1996 John Compton

Photo: André Elbing

1998 Amir Thaleb

Photo: André Elbing

2001 Morocco

2001 Adam Basma

Photo: André Elbing

2003 Gamila

2006 Randa Kamel

2010 Nadia

2012 Dina

Jareeda give special thanks to the following people who helped fund this project on kickstarter.com. Your support is greatly appreciated!

Carol Henning
Brian Thomas
Janice Wing
Denise Gilbertson
Rebecca Wolf-Nail
Teresa Wing
Diana Ernest
Jessica Brown
Brianna Molter
Pat Spark
Donna Lynn Joy
Linda Cox
Roxy Stimpson
Amy Anna
Wendy Campbell
Ginger Mayorga
Sharon Fetter
Amara Nomadeen
Sam McQuiston
Suzanne McNeil
Deborah Rennie
Cheryl Strecker
Judy Smith
Woodrow Jarvis Hill
Jennifer Hawks

Angela Palmer
Karen Gordon
Donna Sullivan
Kandy Sinquefield
Mearah Rose
Deborah Rubin
Morocco (C.V. Dinicu)
Anne Wallace
Saqra Raybuck
Sally Pelkey
Jean Hale
Paolo Tiramani
Zendra Unican Tams
Terri Davis
Suhaila International
Penny Devine
Jewels Barrera
Devi Safir
Betty Adams
Turquoise International
Donna Didi Reyes
Casey
Jonna Wagner
Marilee G. Humason
Lisa Smith

A special thank you goes to Naomi Meacham for helping me edit this beast.

And, special thanks to my dear friend Leila Najma. Her belief in me and encouragement has been invaluable during the past couple of years. She is also a great resource for our dance community. Check out her website. **www.leyla-najma.com** / What an amazing woman!

Made in the USA
Coppell, TX
15 September 2021